A READER IN CULTURE CHANGE

VOLUME I: THEORIES

A READER IN CULTURE CHANGE

VOLUME I: THEORIES

Edited by Ivan A. Brady
and Barry L. Isaac

Schenkman Publishing Company

Halsted Press Division
JOHN WILEY AND SONS
New York – London – Sydney – Toronto

Copyright © 1975
Schenkman Publishing Company
3 Mount Auburn Place
Cambridge, Mass. 02138

Distributed solely by Halsted Press, a Division
of John Wiley & Sons, Inc. New York.

Library of Congress Cataloging in Publication Data

Brady, Ivan A.   comp.
    A reader in culture change.

    Bibliography: v. 1., p.
    CONTENTS: v. 1. Theories. — v. 2. Case studies

1. Social evolution — Addresses, essays, lectures.
2. Acculturation — Addresses, essays, lectures.
3. Social change — Addresses, essays, lectures.
I. Isaac, Barry L., joint comp. II. Title.
GN320.B69   301.24   73-2231
ISBN 0-470-09532-6 (set)

CONTENTS

VOLUME I: THEORIES

The two volumes of A Reader In Culture Change are
available separately, and also in a clothbound edition
bound together as one book. Volume II, the *Case Studies*,
presents papers and articles on The Contact of Cultures,
and on Cultural Engineering.

To Homer G. Barnett,
Mentor and Friend

ACKNOWLEDGEMENTS

We acknowledge with appreciation the promptness and generosity of the authors and publishers who have given us permission to reprint the essays in this anthology. The Graduate School of the University of Cincinnati provided a small grant to help defray production costs. Several students have read these materials and offered comments on matters of content and organization; we especially thank Mark Westrich and Kenneth Rawlings in this regard. Other students, Sue Perkins Taylor, Charles Mooar helped compile the bibliographies. Gloria Bowman diligently assisted with the typing. We have had the pleasure of being assisted at every step in the production process by Sheila Segal, Timothy Cuerdon, and Alfred Schenkman of Schenkman Publishing Company. Finally, we acknowledge with deepest appreciation the cooperation and assistance of Janie Brady and Rosalea Hostetler.

INTRODUCTION

Social scientists have studied culture change from a variety of viewpoints in many of the world's societies. The combined efforts of economists, historians, political scientists, psychologists, sociologists and anthropologists have produced a substantial body of literature on the subject. However, the search for order in the diverse data covered by these disciplines has not always yielded compatible results, in part because of differences in research focus, and in part because of inadequate methods and theories. Even within particular disciplines, the generalizations made about culture change often are contradictory (see especially Kushner, *et al.* 1962). If anything bordering on the absolute can be said at the present time concerning this kaleidoscope of methods, theories, and facts it is that social scientists have only begun to realize the complexities of human cultures and how they change. The "state of the art" at present is that important questions about culture change far outnumber reliable answers.

An interest in comparative methods and worldwide samples of cultures has led anthropologists in particular to ask: What generates particular kinds of cultural responses to changing physical and cultural environments? Why do these responses variously persist, diffuse, transmute, or die out at apparently variable rates in ostensibly similar settings? Why do we encounter the strikingly large number of cross-cultural similarities in such things as monumental architecture, material exchange patterns, kinship organization, beliefs in celestial beings, and so on, amidst the otherwise apparent diversity of human cultures? Is technology the prime-mover of cultural evolution? What is the role of the individual in culture change? Where do we search for laws of cultural stability and change?

To answer these and other important questions on a satisfactory scientific level we must have a consistent and productive body of method and theory. We must be able to isolate the principles that guide particular cultures in one direction or another, and our studies must be of sufficient scope overall to present a viable sample of the world's cultures through time. We must be able to identify the cultural and ecological processes that produce the facts of culture change, ideally under all possible combinations of circumstances. Of course, all of this presumes some knowledge of the nature of culture itself. Progress toward each of these goals has generated considerable debate in the last few decades.

Most anthropologists view culture in general as the sum total of beliefs, rules, techniques, institutions, and artifacts that characterize human populations. It is generally agreed that man's ability to symbolize and communicate experience in a formal and abstract manner is the vehicle for all cultural behavior. It is this particular ability that allows man to engineer, stabilize, and perpetuate elaborate social relationships; it enables man to manufacture complex tools, build monuments, calculate history, find gods in foxholes, and otherwise make sense of himself and his environment. In fact, culture may be defined explicitly as "the ordered system of symbols and meanings through which human beings interpret their experience and guide their actions" (Geertz 1957:33). By this definition, social structure becomes the "actually existing network of social relations," and such things as specific norms, institutions, and material artifacts become cultural products or results rather than primary components of culture per se (see Geertz 1957, 1966; Goodenough 1964, 1971; Schneider 1968). Such distinctions, however, are not always acceptable or useful to some observers (see Harris 1968; White and Dillingham 1973).

Discounting philosophical concerns over the nature of cultural versus non-cultural phenomena (see Kroeber and Kluckhohn 1952; Geertz 1962; Harris 1964), most disagreements over definitions of culture are pragmatic. Within certain logical and empirical limits, the definition of culture chosen or constructed by the observer depends to a large extent on the nature of the problem or theory to be investigated. Variations on this level derive from a simple but important pragmatism: like any other analytical constructs, definitions of culture should be revised or discarded when they cease to be useful or theoretically productive. Similar premises and assumptions frame the scope of inquiries into the nature of culture change, of course, and the discovery of how cultures change necessarily reflects back on our understanding of the nature of culture itself.

During the first half of this century, American anthropologists insisted that the search for general laws of culture change must await the detailed study of the history of particular cultures that exist today or have existed in the past. This school of thought is usually associated with Franz Boas, the founder of university based anthropology in the United States, and his many students (including Margaret Mead, Melville Herskovits, Robert Lowie, Alfred Kroeber, among others). Their approach was so firmly grounded in empiricism and delayed by delivery of the facts that it was largely atheoretical. Harris (1968:250-318) refers to this approach as "Historical Particularism." To a great extent, the stance of Boas and his early students was a reaction against the grandiose, speculative, evolutionary schemes of such nineteenth century scholars as Lewis Henry Morgan, Edward B. Tylor, Herbert Spencer, and others. To our knowledge, no one ever faulted Boas and his students for their insistence that armchair speculation is a poor substitute for ethnographic field work. But many critics have argued—and rightly, we feel—that Boas and his students threw the proverbial baby out with the bath. Not only did they eschew evolutionism to such an extent that the very word came to be regarded as heretical, even subversive, in the field, but they also suspended the ". . . normal dialectic between fact and theory" (Harris 1968:251) that characterizes scientific endeavor. They failed to acknowledge that the data do not "speak for themselves," but must, rather, be interpreted theoretically.

The study of broad-scale evolutionary processes did not make a substantial comeback in anthropology until the 1950s and 1960s. Its return marked the rise of a new school, often referred to as the "Michigan School," because it was and is identified largely with Leslie A. White and his students (including Elman Service, Marshall Sahlins, Robert Carneiro, Betty Meggers, among others) at the University of Michigan. Their stance as regards the Historical Particularists is perhaps best summed up by White's statement (1959b:18) that "the opponents of cultural evolutionism were confusing the culture history of peoples with evolutionary sequences of culture." This distinction has been mapped out clearly and cast in a productive theoretical framework by Sahlins and Service (1960) in their discussion of general and specific evolution.

To Boas and his students, cultural anthropology was essentially the study of the ". . . psychology of the peoples of the world" (Boas 1911: 63; available in Hymes 1964). The purpose of field anthropology was to gather explicit data on the natives' own perception of the world (Boas 1911; see also Malinowski 1922, 1926). In other words, any laws of culture change we might eventually discover would be psychological laws. Perhaps the most eloquent and trenchant statement of this position made to date is Homer Barnett's essay, "Laws of Socio-Cultural

Change" (1965). Because cultural phenomena ". . . serve to circumvent, ameliorate, redirect, or nullify the operations and imperatives of natural laws," Barnett argues, they are ". . . particularistic and ad hoc solutions to man's problems," and therefore ". . . exhibit no lawful design" (1965:225). Thus, from a psychological point of view, the loci of change in human behavior and culture are to be found in the areas of cognition, perception, information processing, and symbolic transformations that produce innovations.

The neo-evolutionists, led by White and his students, are concerned exclusively with the supra-individual, non-psychological factors of culture and culture change. To White (1949:181ff), culture is a ". . . vast continuum, a stream of cultural elements. . . . that flows down through time." Technology in its grandest sense is the basis for and determinant of cultural systems: "The motive power of a culture . . . lies in its technology, for here it is that energy is harnessed and put to work" (White 1959b:27). Technology is said to determine the form of social systems, and technology and society together determine the content and orientation of ideology (White 1949:366). Harris (1968:634-687) labels this approach "Cultural Materialism" because it regards as primary the material forces that lie outside of the direct control, or even thorough comprehension, of individuals. White recognizes, of course, that culture could not continue without individuals bound together as societies and groups; but he does not consider ". . . man at all—as a species, race, or individual—*in an explanation* of culture change" (White 1949:181; emphasis in original). Culture from this point of view is explainable only in terms that transcend particular individuals, cognition, shared ideas, or psychological processes in general. Culture is conceived as a total configuration of human beliefs, behaviors, institutions, and tools; but, the Materialist argues, the persistence, decline, or transformation of these elements is predicated on adaptive forces that are expressed primarily through technology (see also Steward 1955).

Some middle ground between these psychological and technological extremes is held by Clifford Geertz (1963), who, in viewing man as an actor in an ecosystem, is careful not to assign prepotency to psychological processes such as innovation, to cross-cultural processes of diffusion, or to ecological stimulii in the determination of social alignments and overall culture content in particular groups. He argues persuasively that propositions about the source of culture change need proof rather than mere assertion (1963:11), and that there is no valid reason to assume in advance that any single factor will be of overriding importance in determining the organization and content of culture in a given society. This approach allows for a dialectic or cumulative feedback relationship among ecological stimulii, cognition, and social action in all aspects of culture and culture change. The theoretical underpinning of techno-environmental determinism as *the* prime-mover of culture change is dismissed as a "prejudice" (1963:11). Nevertheless, at some point documentation of the facts and processes of culture change in particular groups must give way to higher-level theory, and controversy on this higher level of analysis is a healthy and perhaps necessary stage in our development of laws of culture change.

II

The editing of any book of readings involves difficult decisions of inclusion and exclusion. For two reasons, these selection problems seem particularly acute in the case of an introductory reader in culture change. First, the literature on the subject is vast, posing mechanical problems in coverage. Second, as outlined above, opinion on the subject is polarized in anthropology to the extent that any selection an editor makes is bound to be damned in some quarters and praised in others, for a variety of reasons. We have not attempted to resolve these issues here, for that is not the purpose of these two books. Rather, we have tried to make selections that represent as many different viewpoints and problems as space allows. We have also made selections on the premise that students read with greater appreciation and enthusiasm a collection of essays that covers theoretical as well as descriptive case materials.

This volume is devoted to theories of culture change. All of the essays in it touch directly or indirectly on the major theories that have been offered by anthropologists concerning the impact of the individual on culture change and the mechanisms of cultural evolution. The opening section leaves the role of the individual in culture change largely unresolved, for that is the way the issue stands in the social sciences today. Two of the essays in the second section, those by Service and Isaac, pursue the nagging doubt that there may not be any one mechanism that is everywhere *the* prime-mover of cultural evolution. Some of these essays have been written by scholars from fields other than anthropology. Copeland, for example, is a philosopher, as was Plekhanov. Ogburn was a sociologist. Maxim was an engineer. Each of these essays pertains to one or more important theoretical problems that ramify throughout the study of culture change by social scientists.

Volume II is devoted primarily to case studies of culture change. As in the preceding volume, not all of the essays were written by anthropologists: Croizier is an historian, Wharton is an economist, and Underwood is a nutritionist. The first section of Volume II merits special attention because the diffusion of elements through cross-cultural contact is one of the major mechanisms of culture change everywhere, both from the short-term and the long-term points of view. The authors in this section focus variously on social, economic, political, and religious changes that have resulted from cross-cultural contacts in many parts of the world.

The second section of Volume II concerns some of the problems and prospects of cultural engineering—a special type of culture change in which the bearers of one culture consciously attempt to alter the cultural profile of another group. This is the domain of "applied research" programs in general, and, in a more specific sense, the domain of foreign aid, the Peace Corps, and a variety of domestic development schemes, such as VISTA in the United States. The range of such programs in the modern world is great, and their failure rate, in terms of both intended and unintended consequences, is very high. The essays by Patch and Wellin in particular illustrate the genuine need for greater groundwork in the study of culture and culture change as a prerequisite to such programs. A rethinking of the morality and ethics of remaking other cultures in the administrators' own image, and of the responsibilities of social science researchers in general, is also in order, as Beals points out. Croizier's essay deals with a particular problem of internal cultural engineering on a national scale in China. Gross and Underwood detail some of the unexpected consequences of the introduction of sisal agriculture in Brazil. The final essay, by Wharton, concerns some of the unexpected responsibilities and repercussions of the Western world's agricultural revolution as applied to dependent or rural nations.

In both volumes we have introduced each selection with a brief headnote on related materials. A concern for accessibility, quality, and overall pertinence has guided our references to other resources. For practical as well as academic reasons, we have referenced articles on culture change in the Bobbs-Merrill Reprint Series in the Social Sciences; these have been cited as "B-M," followed by the index number for each particular reprint. We feel that instructors as well as students will find these additional references useful.

IAB

PART ONE

The Role of the Individual

in Culture Change

Regardless of the way one views culture or culture change, the problem of how cultural elements are synthesized inevitably surfaces. Homer G. Barnett's thesis on this topic is a formidable statement that identifies the crucial processes and key variables involved in innovations. The points made by Barnett in the following essay ramify throughout both volumes of this Reader in a variety of contexts. We recommend that the student return to Barnett's essay for vital points of contrast and elaboration after reading the remainder of the essays in this anthology. Especially pertinent for additional reading or discussion are Barnett's Innovation *(1953) and his essay on "Laws of Sociocultural Change" (1965).*

One: 1

Invention

Homer G. Barnett*

. . . every [cultural] trait has a form, a meaning, and a function; or, perhaps better stated, a conceptualization in these terms adds greatly to our meager stock of tools for dealing with the processes of cultural change. Linton (1936:402-411) first formulated these concepts . . . . they are used here as he has defined them.[1]

However, to these three, so it seems, there must be added a fourth variable; namely, the principle of a trait. The principle is the scheme or theme about which the form is organized, and it is an inherent part of both material and non-material traits, as we tacitly recognize when we speak about the principle of the lever, or the principles of matrilineal descent and collective responsibility. The principle is the dynamic aspect of form; that quality or property which manifests itself only when the form is in action. It is the scheme of this action and we may answer the question as to principle by inquiring into the arrangement of parts which is essential to performance. A principle is an operative system or plan and in itself has nothing intrinsically to do with human behavior, although the latter shapes itself about principles. It is advisable to distinguish at once between these operational principles which are action schemes, and still others which might be termed principles of construction.

Linton has discussed the complex interrelations of the different aspects of a trait and we need not go into them here, but it is desirable at this point to stress the importance of the well recognized arbitrary connection between a given form and the meaning-function construc-

*Excerpted from "Invention and Cultural Change," by Homer G. Barnett. Reproduced by permission of the author and the American Anthropological Association from *American Anthropologist*, Vol. 44, No. 1 (1942), 14-30.

Homer G. Barnett is professor emeritus of anthropology at the University of Oregon, where he has taught since 1939.

tion put upon it by a particular culture. This is the crux of the problem, for although objectively all such constructions are arbitrary, once established they take on the quality of inexorable fitness for the members of a society wherein that particular interpretation is the mode; and it is only the extraordinary individual, the inventor, who can dissociate the component elements and envision the possibilities of other combinations. For it is the severance of the traditional form-meaning connection, by reason of an insight into underlying principle, which produces the observed occurrences of different forms having the same function, or the same form having different functions. Furthermore, there is a pattern or formula which yields these alternative associations and so characterizes the process which we call invention.

This conviction stems from an analysis of what has taken place in a wide variety of concrete cases of invention. The material comes from what descriptive matter there is on the subject but even more helpfully from such pictures of original models and statements of purpose and patent coverage (meaning and function) as have been accessible. Every case analyzed conforms to a scheme which can be characterized in terms of either one of two complementary propositions. One of these states that an invention entails an insight into the principle operating in a familiar form and serving a familiar function to the end that the same principle be envisioned and utilized in a new form to serve a new function. Colloquially we might say that here is an old way of doing something different. In effect what results is the same principle operating through two different forms to serve two different functions. Parenthetically, the "new" form in the beginning is usually not new; it is commonly a derivative of the old one, is suggested by it, and in the initial conception is the same form bodily lifted from the old context. This is as clear as can be in the first models of technological inventions; at most the old form at first is only slightly modified to suit the requirements of the new context. It is only later and even then gradually that the new form becomes better adapted to the new function. Any one can testify to this when he reflects upon it.

The other proposition which comprehends the process of an invention states that the inventor through his insight into principle perceives the possibility of utilizing two different principles, already acting through two different but familiar forms, to achieve the same function. Colloquially, this would be a new way of doing the same thing. I have called this the obverse of the first proposition for in all common-run inventions the two are concomitant, one being the complementary aspect of the other. This can easily be appreciated by comparing the two colloquial expressions. Which one is used depends upon the speaker's point of view, and they amount to the same thing. The reason for this is that most inventions are on the one hand suggested by a device already in operation (using the same principle) and on the other hand are intended to be a substitute (an "improvement") for another one also already in operation but using a different principle. Thus the automobile jack using the lever and ratchet principles has long been familiar to car owners and mechanics. More recently there appeared a device serving the same function but necessarily having a different form, for it employed a different principle: the screw jack. This, it seems evident, was suggested by a different form (a vise or compressor) serving entirely different functions. On the one hand this was a principle departure and a functional substitute, and on the other it was a reapplied principle and a functional departure; from the viewpoint of the automobile mechanic it was a new way to do the same thing, from the viewpoint of the bookbinder or carpenter it was an old way to do something different.

This example of the jack brings out a further fact in evidence of the affirmation that the two propositions are complementary, that we are dealing with a unit sequence of borrowing-to-substitute. The mechanic would undoubtedly find the screw jack more familiar than would the carpenter. This is because the inventor anticipated the substitution, and the form to be substituted for dominated his idea of what a jack should look like. The screw jack therefore retained only such differential elements as were requisite to the operation of the new screw pressure principle.

The majority of inventions fall into this pattern and can easily be demonstrated to conform to it. Stated succinctly it is the borrowing of a form and a principle from one functional context for the purpose of substituting them in another context formerly serviced by a different form and principle. That this is psychologically correct is indicated by the telltale character of the borrowed forms of first models. They link one way or the other and show their kinship either with the form with the same principle or with the one for which they are to substitute functionally. There is moreover the obvious and explicit purpose of replacement which in our day stimulates a deliberate hunt for substitutes with the hope that the new form and principle will not only be accepted as a functional equivalent and alternate but will supersede the older device and submerge it in the market.

The validity of the concept must be left to the reader. It can readily be tested on any invention the background of which is known.

Throughout, it is to be noted that the genius of invention lies in disencumbering form of its traditional associations, of seeing it objectively with respect to its active principle and its possibilities for other meanings and functions.

The propositions offered can be diagrammed, and perhaps for the reader as for the writer their character and validity can be revealed to advantage by a presentation of the scheme which has been used in clarifying and handling the abstract relationships embodied in them. They can also be stated in terms of a proportional equation (A:B as X:Y) but this does not give any further insight into the process.

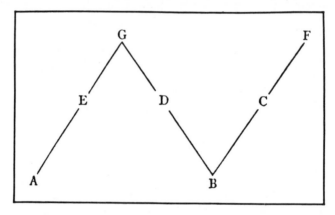

In this diagram A and B symbolize different principles; C, D, and E represent different forms, although D may draw upon either C or E as a model; F and G represent different functions. Each line therefore represents a trait, and the convergence of two of them represents the recognition of a common function for them at G, or of a common principle acting in them at B. Divergence of lines represents different functions at F and G, the traits being connected by a common principle at B, or a difference in principles at A and B connected by a common function at G. Line BCF may be visualized as the borrowing line swinging over to the left on pivot B to create a new invention BDG which then substitutes for an old one AEG.

As said this scheme describes what takes place in the majority of inventions. Let us speak of these as of class A, for there are two variations upon the pattern. Neither requires any new conception; they are essentially the same and conform to the above scheme except that in one case (class B) the trait BCF, the prototype, is missing or not apparent; and in the other (class C) the trait AEG, the one to be substituted for, is either non-existent or perhaps unrealized. In the diagram for the case of class B inventions the line BCF may be thought of as dotted to indicate uncertainty or vagueness, and likewise line AEG for class C; for as we shall see they might correspond to realities only dimly or indirectly appreciated by the inventor, so rendering the pattern of the process not at all different from the regular class A.

Class B inventions are the most remarkable, the most "revolutionizing" ones. The layman stands in awe of them and for a very good psychological reason which harks back to the standard scheme or dual proposition set up. They are striking because they appear to spring up from nowhere; that is, they do not draw upon an existing prototype for a principle. In other words, they rest upon the discovery of a new principle, and for this reason they are more uncommon, call for more experimentation and insight, and in their consequences are more startling. Each such discovery of a principle with its totally new form then follows the familiar pattern of a functional substitution for an old trait (AEG), so that the BDG-AEG part of our diagram still represents the situation. And it is to be noted that this abbreviation of the standard class A pattern occurs only with the initial discovery of a new principle, if at all; for in many instances of initial discovery the principle has long been in operation in some form in nature, and this may provide the inventor with a prototype and an inspiration. At other times a principle is discovered in a fortuitously created form which then becomes the prototype.

It remains to be suggested that many striking inventions at first glance appear to belong to this class B category but actually do not. That is, they do not depend upon the discovery of a new principle but only simulate this since they utilize a well-known principle but in reverse action. Thus the circulation of water can be utilized either to heat a radiator or to cool a gasoline engine; the reciprocating piston either to compress air or to drive a locomotive; the propeller either to pull an airplane or to cool a room; the hydraulic piston either to press pulp or to lift an elevator; the water wheel either to drive a mill or a steam boat; the electro-magnetic field either to drive a street car as a motor, or to generate electricity or light as a dynamo. In all these pairs the principle is the same and the function depends merely upon which end of the machine is tied down so to speak.

We may now turn to the class C inventions, and if of class B we can say that they take greater insight than A, of this class we might say that they take greater foresight—or foolhardiness, which often amounts to the same thing. For in these cases the left arm of our diagram is missing or dotted, which, culturally interpreted, means that there is nothing which they aim at displacing, or at least nothing obvious. This means in turn that no need is felt for them and they are strays looking for a function. They are definitely the queers among inventions variously called fantastic, ridiculous, inane, useless, or ahead of their time. The magazine *Time* periodically makes a sardonic report of these vagaries. Listed in the July 29, 1940 issue, p. 42, are, among others, these patented inventions: women's shoes which can be raised or lowered by a screw operated jack in the heels; a golf putter equipped with a two handled grip and a leveling gauge; a non-slip crutch with three legs instead of one; an electrically heated toilet seat; a wind driven wagon with wind vanes mounted on the wheels; and an apparatus which wakes a drowsing motorist by blowing ammonia vapor in his face when he relaxes his grip on the wheel.

Although I have no precise information to offer on the inspirations for these inventions, I think that they bear in themselves sufficient evidence as to their character. A prototype trait (BCF) employing the same principle to meet a diverse need is obviously operative in every case: for the shoes, any one of several things, perhaps a car jack; for the golf club, a carpenter's or other level; for the crutch, some tripod arrangement as for cameras, transits, etc; for the motorist, a spray atomizer of various descriptions and purposes; for the toilet seat, a warming pad, etc. As for the existence or non-existence of the traits (AEG) employing a different principle and form for which these might substitute it can be said that a case can be made out for their existence in every instance, but for some the construction might seem fantastic. The golf club level, for example, might be construed to be a functional equivalent and substitute for human muscular coordination; or the toilet seat for human body warmth; or the lady's shoe for several pairs of shoes of different heights. But this last construction is not so preposterous, and with it we begin to grade into those cases in which real AEG traits exist. Thus the ammonia vapor awakener clearly offers a substitute for the different principles operating in the different forms (pills, drinks, etc.) now offered on the market for keeping the motorist awake. In this instance therefore we have the standard class A pattern. Likewise the pills in their turn conform to the standard pattern, the trait they substituted for being the common custom of drinking coffee and other stimulants to keep awake. But with this, that is coffee, we seem to have reached again a class C innovation; for the only thing it appears to substitute for is human will power and endurance.

This gives a clue for a refinement of our concepts and leads to an interesting inference. It will be observed that unqualified instances of inventions of either class B or class C are comparatively rare, and that both kinds grade into the larger class A pattern. It will be remembered further that the characteristic of an undoubted class B invention is the discovery of a new principle. This means that it does not draw upon any antecedent *culture trait.* It does however draw upon nature, that is, upon the inherent consistencies of the physical world on the one hand and—until it can be shown otherwise—upon the inherent qualities of social living on the other. The complement of this kind of an invention, as has already been pointed out, belongs to class C. These constructions have been characterized as being non-substitutional. But the analysis in the preceding paragraph points to this refinement: that while they do not substitute for any culture trait, they can be characterized specifically by the fact that they substitute for what have previously been functions of the physical and mental equipment of the human machine. This makes it easier to understand why a toilet seat warmer, for example, sounds so ludicrous, and why the Rube Goldberg "inventions" of a few years ago appeared where they did; namely, in the funny papers. The notion of an invention to lift a man's fork to his mouth, or to put him to bed, or to do his thinking for him is mildly funny if not absurd. Still this has been the course of development of the whole of culture. From one point of view the essential nature of culture is that it modifies the direct expression of man's innate physical and mental equipment by interposing a complex nexus of auxiliary and intermediary mechanisms between him and his natural and social environment.

Perhaps it will have occurred to the reader that there is logically one further possible combination of our four variables which has not yet been mentioned. This would result from the development of a new form using the same principle and serving the same function. Diagrammed, this set of relationships would look like a diamond. If we are correct in the preceding analysis, this fact alone should suggest to us that in this case we are not dealing with an invention. But we need not put our trust in such a rule of thumb demonstration. For it will become apparent upon reflection that here we are dealing with an entirely different phenomenon, both psychologically and culturally. The product is certainly something new, but it is new only in its formal aspects. The rest is as familiar as can be. The newness lies solely in formal modification and elaboration, and with this development we enter the domain of art. In this the ingenious and fanciful play with line, tone, color, and material comes into its own, for it is distinctly the artist who strives after oddity, singularity, and uniqueness of form. But if the object, institution, or behavior is to retain its original function and principle, there is quite definitely a limit to such imaginative embellishments on the bald "practical" form. Thus a vessel for holding cut flowers can vary almost infinitely in form, but it must retain the essential qualities which give expression to the principle involved; it must be a watertight container with an opening at the top. The material can vary from any metal to any natural or any synthetic product, the shape from a plate to a globe with holes for the insertion of flower stems, the color at will, and so forth. The material objects of our daily life practically all bear witness to this process of artistic formal modification, and although the elaboration may seem to be without stint it requires only a little thought to see that it must confine itself to the limits prescribed by function and just as inescapably by principle.

Since we are not given to thinking in such terms, it may smack of dogmatism to insist that institutions and behaviors conform to this interpretation. If so, it would seem that its validity would be demonstrated beyond doubt if we can show that certain of our so-called art forms—prime media for gifted expression—bear out the argument. I believe that even in the so-called fine arts, as opposed to the applied, it is a commonplace that there are inviolable principles; that these can be taught; and furthermore, that they must be learned before an artist can try his wings. This is inspiration within bounds; it is inspiration with respect to form, not principle or function. The amateur poet or sculptor who thinks that art is simply an expression of self must soon find out differently. The existence of these principles, which are analogous to the utility requirements in the applied arts, is the only justification for art schools, since admittedly talent, that is, ingenuity in formal manipulation, cannot be taught. To take but one illustration I think it cannot be denied that the novel is built around, that is, embodies as an essential part of its form, certain principles. We call these plots. There are a limited number of these and all of the play of artistic fancy and ingenuity is bent toward disguising this fact. This then is the field of art and the artist cannot overstep these boundaries by too great a formal elaboration without adulterating or doing violence to the plot and so altering the function of the story. Of course it is possible for a writer to envision the possibility of utilizing the same plot (principle) to serve a new function, and this has been done. There was a man one day, probably long before stories came to be written, who in this wise saw the possibility of using a story for propaganda purposes instead of as a vehicle for amusement, vicarious enjoyment, or escape from reality, and as a substitute for the cruder technique (principle) of haranguing. This man was an inventor, no less. . . . He was not using the same principle in a different form for the same function, which is what we are here considering and calling art. It seems therefore that there is some real justification for holding propaganda as a suspect art form, for the propagandist tries to obscure functions through simulating an art or information form or medium; and the hold which form has upon minds in determining meaning is the fact which contributes to his purpose.

This illustration also demonstrates very neatly . . . that artistic elaboration may so completely obscure the primary, idea-in-mind principle as to render it problematical and afford the objective observer with grounds for seeing embodied in the form other principles allowing of other functions. The observer then, from the *artist's* viewpoint, but not from his own, would be an inventor. Relayed into functional terms, which is the way in which we think of these things, all of us are familiar with such ambiguities. The propagandist plays upon this possibility; and if our modern designer is outraged when we naively confuse his formal evening creation with a negligee, or his "functional" floor lamp with a hat rack, he may temper his exasperation with the consolation that this is a common human failing not totally devoid of creativeness.

NOTE

[1]Briefly, the "form" of a trait is how it looks to the observer; its "meaning" is what people think or feel about it; while its "function" is what it does for the people and their culture (see Barnett 1940:31n).

In 1898, the Russian philosopher Georg Plekhanov, writing under the pen name of A. Kirsanov, published a brief essay on "The Role of the Individual in History." Plekhanov intended his essay as an attack on those opponents of Marxism who branded it a sterile doctrine that denied the significance of individuals in the development of society. The first six chapters are devoted largely to squabbles within the Movement at that time; as such, they are of interest to non-Marxist scholars largely as historical documents. In contrast, Chapters 7 and 8, which are reprinted here in slightly abridged form, are of lasting interest to all students of historical processes. These two short chapters are an eloquent commentary on what has come to be known as the "Great Man Theory of History," which purports to explain historical events in terms of individual generals, politicians, clerics, diplomats—and of what they ate or drank, how they felt, or to whom they talked or made love at particular times and places. Plekhanov's approach to the study of history was not essentially different from the "superorganic" approach of the great American anthropologist Alfred L. Kroeber or the "culturology" of Leslie A. White (see Selection One: 3, this volume).

For lecture or discussion of Plekhanov's essay, we recommend both Kroeber's "The Superorganic" (1917; B-M, S-154) and White's delightfully sarcastic "Ikhnaton: The Great Man vs. the Culture Process" (White 1949:233-281).

One: 2

The Role of the Individual in History

*Georg Plekhanov**

. . . In discussing the role great men play in history, we nearly always fall victims to a sort of optical illusion. . . .

In coming out in the role of the "good sword" to save public order, Napoleon prevented all the other generals from playing this role, and some of them might have performed it in the same way, or almost the same way, as he did. Once the public need for an energetic military ruler was satisfied, the social organization barred the road to the position of military ruler for all other talented soldiers. Its power became a power that was unfavorable to the appearance of other talents of a similar kind. This is the cause of the optical illusion, which we have mentioned. Napoleon's personal power presents itself to us in an extremely magnified form, for we place to his account the social power which had brought him to the front and supported him. Napoleon's power appears to us to be something quite exceptional because the other powers similar to it did not pass from the potential to the real. And when we are asked, "What would have happened if there had been no Napoleon?" our *imagination* becomes confused and it seems to us that without him the social movement upon which his power and influence were based could not have taken place.

In the history of the development of human intellect, the success of some individual hinders the success of another individual much more rarely. But even here we are not free from the above-mentioned optical illusion. When a given state of society sets certain problems before its intellectual representatives, the attention of prominent minds is concentrated upon them until these problems are solved. As soon as they have succeeded in solving them, their attention is transferred to an-

*Chapters VII and VIII of *The Role of the Individual in History,* by Georg Plekhanov, pp. 49-62. Reprinted by permission of International Publishers Co., Inc. Copyright © 1940.

other object. By solving a problem a given talent A diverts the attention of talent B from the problem already solved to another problem.
And when we are asked: What would have happened if A had died before
he had solved problem X?—we imagine that the thread of development of the human intellect would have been broken. We forget that
had A died B, or C, or D might have tackled the problem, and the
thread of intellectual development would have remained intact in
spite of A's premature demise.

In order that a man who possesses a particular kind of talent may, by
means of it, greatly influence the course of events, two conditions are
needed: First, this talent must make him more conformable to the
social needs of the given epoch than anyone else. If Napoleon had
possessed the musical gifts of Beethoven instead of his own military
genius he would not, of course, have become an emperor. Second, the
existing social order must not bar the road to the person possessing
the talent which is needed and useful precisely at the given time. This
very *Napoleon* would have died as the barely known General, or
Colonel, *Bonaparte* had the older order in France existed another
seventy-five years.[1] In 1789, Davout, Désaix, Marmont and MacDonald
were subalterns; Bernadotte was a *sergeant-major;* Hoche, Marceau,
Lefebre, Pichegru, Ney, Masséna, Murat and Soult were *non-com-
missioned officers;* Augereau was a *fencing master;* Lannes was a *dyer;*
Gouvion Saint-Cyr was an *actor;* Jourdan was a *peddler;* Bessières
was a *barber;* Brune was a *compositor;* Joubert and Junot were *law
students;* Kléber was an *architect;* Martier did not see any military service until the Revolution.

Had the old order continued to exist up to our days it would never
have occurred to any of us that in France, at the end of the last century,[2] certain actors, compositors, barbers, dyers, lawyers, peddlers
and fencing masters had been potential military geniuses.[3]

Stendhal observed that a man who was born at the same time as
Titian, in 1477, could have lived forty years with Raphael, who died
in 1520, and with Leonardo da Vinci, who died in 1519; that he could
have spent many years with Corregio, who died in 1534, and with
Michelangelo, who lived until 1563; that he would have been no
more than thirty-four years of age when Giorgione died; that he could
have been acquainted with Tintoretto, Bassano, Veronese, Julian
Romano and Andrea del Sarto; that, in short, he would have been
the contemporary of all the great painters, with the exception of those
who belonged to the Bologna School, which arose a full century later.
Similarly, it may be said that a man who was born in the same year as

Wouwermann could have been personally acquainted with nearly all the great Dutch painters; and a man of the same age as Shakespeare would have been the contemporary of a number of remarkable playwrights.

It has long been observed that great talents appear everywhere, whenever the social conditions favorable to their development exist. This means that every man of talent who *actually appears*, every man of talent who becomes a *social force*, is the product of *social relations*. Since this is the case, it is clear why talented people can, as we have said, change only individual features of events, but not their general trend; *they are themselves the product of this trend; were is not for that trend they would never have crossed the threshold that divides the potential from the real.*

It goes without saying that there is talent and talent. "When a fresh step in the development of civilization calls into being a new form of art," rightly says Taine, "scores of talents which only half express social thought appear around one or two geniuses who express it perfectly" (Taine 1863:I:5). If, owing to certain mechanical or physiological causes unconnected with the general course of the social-political and intellectual development of Italy, Raphael, Michelangelo and Leonardo da Vinci had died in their infancy, Italian art would have been less perfect, but the general trend of its development in the period of the Renaissance would have remained the same. Raphael, Leonardo da Vinci and Michelangelo did not create this trend; they were merely its best representatives. True, usually a whole school springs up around a man of genius, and his pupils try to copy his methods to the minutest details; that is why the gap that would have been left in Italian art in the period of the Renaissance by the early death of Raphael, Michelangelo and Leonardo da Vinci would have strongly influenced many of the secondary features of its subsequent history. But in essence, there would have been no change in this history, provided there were no important changes in the general course of the intellectual development of Italy due to general causes.

It is well known, however, that quantitative differences ultimately pass into qualitative differences. This is true everywhere, and is therefore true in history. A given trend in art may remain without any remarkable expression if an unfavorable combination of circumstances carries away, one after the other, several talented people who might have given it expression. But the premature death of such talented people can prevent the artistic expression of this trend only if it is too shallow to produce new talent. As, however, the depth of any given trend in literature and art is determined by its importance for the class, or stratum, whose tastes it expresses, and by the social role played by that class or stratum, here, too, in the last analysis, everything depends upon the course of social development and on the relation of social forces.

Thus, the personal qualities of leading people determine the individual features of historical events; and the accidental element, in the sense that we have indicated, always plays some role in the course of these events, the trend of which is determined, in the last analysis, by so-called general causes, *i.e.*, actually by the development of productive forces and the mutual relations between men in the social-economic process of production. Casual phenomena and the personal qualities of celebrated people are ever so much more noticeable than deep-lying general causes. The eighteenth century pondered but little over these general causes, and claimed that history was explained by the conscious actions and "passions" of historical personages. The philosophers of that century asserted that history might have taken an entirely different course as a result of the most insignificant causes; for example, if some "atom" had started playing pranks in some ruler's head (an idea expressed more than once in *Système de la Nature*).

The adherents of the new trend in the science of history began to argue that history could not have taken any other course than the one it has taken, notwithstanding all "atoms." Striving to emphasize the effect of general causes as much as possible, they ignored the personal qualities of historical personages. According to their arguments, historical events would not have been affected in the least by the substitution of some persons for others, more or less capable.[4] But if we make such an assumption then we must admit that the *personal element is of no significance whatever in history*, and that everything can be reduced to the operation of general causes, to the general laws of historical progress. This would be going to an extreme which leaves no room for the particle of truth contained in the opposite opinion. It is precisely for this reason that the opposite opinion retained some right to existence. The collision between these two opinions assumed the form of an antinomy, the first part of which was general laws, and the second part was the activities of individuals. From the point of view of the second part of the antinomy, history was simply a chain of accidents; from the point of view of the first part it seemed that even the individual features of historical events were determined by the operation of general causes. But if the individual features of events are determined by the influence of general causes and do not depend upon the personal qualities of historical personages, it follows that these features are *determined by general causes* and cannot be changed, no matter how much these personages may change. Thus, the theory assumes a *fatalistic* character.

This did not escape the attention of its opponents. Sainte-Beuve compared Mignet's conception of history with that of Bossuet. Bossuet thought that the force which causes historical events to take place comes from above, that events serve to express the divine will. Mignet sought for this force in the human passions, which are displayed in historical events as inexorably and immutably as the forces of nature. But both regarded history as a chain of phenomena which could not have been different, no matter under what circumstances; both were fatalists; in this respect, the philosopher was not far removed from the priest (*le philosophe se rapproache du prêtre*).

This reproach was justified as long as the doctrine that social phenomena conformed to certain laws, reduced the influence of the personal qualities of prominent historical individuals to a cipher. And the impression made by this reproach was all the more strong for the reason that the historians of the new school, like the historians and philosophers of the eighteenth century, regarded *human nature* as a higher instance, from which all the *general causes* of historical movement sprang, and to which they were subordinated. As the French Revolution had shown that historical events are not determined by the *conscious* actions of men alone, Mignet and Guizot, and the other historians of the same trend, put in the forefront the effect of *passions*, which often rebelled against all control of the mind. But if passions are the final and most general cause of historical events, then why is Sainte-Beuve wrong in asserting that the outcome of the French Revolution might have been the opposite of what we know it was if there had been individuals capable of imbuing the French people with passions opposite to those which had excited them? Mignot would have said: Because other passions could not have excited the French people at that time owing to the very qualities of human nature. In a certain sense this would have been true. But this truth would have had a strongly fatalistic tinge, for it would have been on a par with the thesis that the history of mankind, in all its details, is pre-determined by the *general* qualities of human nature. Fatalism would have appeared here as the result of the disappearance of the *individual in the general.* Incidentally, it is always the result of such a disappearance. It is said: "If all social phenomena are inevitable, then our activities cannot have any significance." This is a correct idea wrongly formulated. We ought to say: if everything occurs as a result of the *general*, then the *individual*, including my efforts, is of no significance. *This* deduction is correct; but it is incorrectly employed. It is meaningless when applied to the modern materialist conception of history, in which there is room also for the *individual*. But it was justified when applied to the views of the French historians in the period of the Restoration.

At the present time, human nature can no longer be regarded as the final and most general cause of historical progress: if it is constant, then it cannot explain the extremely changeable course of history; if it is changeable, then obviously its changes are themselves determined by historical progress. At the present time we must regard the development of productive forces as the final and most general cause of the historical progress of mankind, and it is these productive forces that determine the consecutive changes in the social relations of men. Parallel with this *general* cause there are *particular* causes, *i.e., the historical situation* in which the development of the productive forces of a given nation proceeds and which, in the last analysis, is itself created by the development of these forces among other nations, *i.e.,* the same general cause.

Finally, the influence of the *particular* causes is supplemented by the operation of *individual* causes, *i.e.,* the personal qualities of public men and other "accidents," thanks to which events finally assume their *individual features*. Individual causes cannot bring about fundamental changes in the operation of *general and particular* causes which, moreover, determine the trend and limits of the influence of individual causes. Nevertheless, there is no doubt that history would have had different features had the individual causes which had influenced it been replaced by other causes of the same order.

Monod and Lamprecht still adhere to the human nature point of view. Lamprecht has categorically, and more than once, declared that in his opinion social mentality is the fundamental cause of historical phenomena. This is a great mistake, and as a result of this mistake the desire, very laudable in itself, to take into account the sum total of social life may lead only to vapid eclecticism or, among the most consistent, to Kabritz's arguments concerning the relative significance of the mind and the senses.

But let us return to our subject. A great man is great not because his personal qualities give individual features to great historical events, but because he possesses qualities which make him most capable of serving the great social needs of his time, needs which arose as a result

A READER IN CULTURE CHANGE

VOLUME I: THEORIES

of general and particular causes. Carlyle, in his well-known book on heroes and hero-worship, calls great men *beginners.* This is a very apt description. A great man is precisely a beginner because he sees *further* than others, and desires things *more strongly* than others. He solves the scientific problems brought up by the preceding process of intellectual development of society; he points to the new social needs created by the preceding development of social relationships; he takes the initiative in satisfying these needs. He is a hero. But he is not a hero in the sense that he can stop, or change, the natural course of things, but in the sense that his activities are the conscious and free expression of this inevitable and unconscious course. Herein lies all his significance; herein lies his whole power. But this significance is colossal, and the power is terrible.

Bismarck said that we cannot make history and must wait while it is being made. But who makes history? It is made by the *social man,* who is its *sole "factor."* The social man creates his own, social, relationships. But if in a given period he creates given relationships and not others, there must be some cause for it, of course; it is determined by the state of his productive forces. No great man can foist on society relations which *no longer* conform to the state of these forces, or which *do not yet* conform to them. In this sense, indeed, he cannot make history, and in this sense he would advance the hands of his clock in vain; he would not hasten the passage of time, nor turn it back. Here Lamprecht is quite right: even at the height of his power Bismarck could not cause Germany to revert to natural economy.

Social relationships have their inherent logic: as long as people live in given mutual relationships they will feel, think and act in a given way, and no other. Attempts on the part of public men to combat this logic would also be fruitless; the natural course of things (this logic of social relationships) would reduce all his effort to nought. But if I know in what direction social relations are changing owing to given changes in the social-economic process of production, I also know in what direction social mentality is changing; consequently, I am able to influence it. Influencing social mentality means influencing historical events. Hence, in a certain sense, I *can make history,* and there is no need for me to wait while "it is being made."

Monod believes that really important events and individuals in history are important only as signs and symbols of the development of institutions and economic conditions. This is a correct although very inexactly expressed idea; but precisely because this idea is correct it is wrong to oppose the activities of great men to "the *slow progress"* of the conditions and institutions mentioned. The more or less slow changes in "economic conditions" periodically confront society with the necessity of more or less rapidly changing its institutions. This change never takes place "by itself"; it always needs the intervention of *men,* who are thus confronted with great social problems. And it is those men who do more than others to facilitate the solution of these problems who are called great men. But *solving a problem* does not mean being only a "symbol" and a "sign" of the fact that it has been solved.

We think that Monod opposed the one to the other mainly because he was carried away by the pleasant catchword, *"slow."* Many modern evolutionists are very fond of this catchword. *Psychologically,* this passion is comprehensible: it *inevitably* arises in the respectable milieu of moderation and punctiliousness. . . . But *logically* it does not bear examination, as Hegel proved.

And it is not only for "beginners," not only for "great" men that a broad field of activity is open. It is open for all those who have eyes to see, ears to hear and hearts to love their neighbors. The concept *great* is a relative concept. In the ethical sense every ·man is great who, to use the Biblical phrase, "lays down his life for his friend."

NOTES

[1]Probably Napoleon would have gone to Russia, *where he had intended to go just a few years before the Revolution.* Here, no doubt, he would have distinguished himself in action against the Turks or the Caucasian highlanders, but nobody here would have thought that this poor, but capable, officer could, under favorable circumstances, have become the ruler of the world.

[2]Terburg, Brower and Rembrandt were born in 1608; Adrian Van-Ostade and Ferdinand Bol were born in 1610; Van der Hölst and Gerard Dow were born in 1615; Wouwermann was born in 1620; Werniks, Everdingen and Painaker were born in 1621; Bergham was born in 1624 and Paul Potter in 1629; Jan Steen was born in 1626; Ruisdal and Metsu were born in 1630; Van der Haiden was born in 1637; Hobbema was born in 1638 and Adrian Van der Velde was born in 1639.

[3]"Shakespeare, Beaumont, Fletcher, Jonson, Webster, Massinger, Ford, Middleton and Heywood, who appeared at the same time, or following each other, represented the new generation which, owing to its favorable position, flourished on the soil which had been prepared by the efforts of the preceding generation" (Taine 1863:I:468).

[4]According to their argument, *i.e.,* when they began to discuss the tendency of historical events to conform to laws. When, however, some of them simply described these phenomena, they sometimes ascribed even exaggerated significance to the personal element. What interests us now, however, are not their descriptions, but their arguments.

As we noted in the Introduction to this volume, Leslie A. White is the founder of the so-called Michigan School of anthropology. Professor White argues that in the man and culture equation, man is the dependent, culture the independent variable. The individual is born into a culture, which molds him in the image appropriate to his society; the belief that the individual molds culture—through free will, education, or social science—stems from man's ignorance of the nature of culture. The belief in man's control over civilization, White argues, is as naive as the belief of our primitive ancestors in their ability to control the weather or the fertility of their habitat through magic. Is this a "fatalistic," "defeatist" philosophy? Professor White argues that it is not, and that "it is only the inveterate habit of thinking anthropocentrically that makes this point of view seem strange."

Although "Man's Control Over Civilization" was first published more than twenty years ago, the questions it raises concerning our ability to influence the course of our own culture are still provocative. In fact, the essay may be even more timely now than it was two decades ago, in view of the recent surge of social activism on a variety of political and economic fronts.

A stimulating complement to White's essay is Crane Brinton's now classic The Anatomy of Revolution (1952), which concludes that even a period of revolutionary turmoil does not radically alter the cultural patterns of a society. A further exposition of White's culturology is his "The Concept of Culture" (1959a; B-M, A-238). For a recent, easy-to-read statement, see White and Dillingham (1973).

One: 3

Man's Control Over Civilization: An Anthropocentric Illusion

*Leslie A. White**

". . . numerous survivals of the anthropocentric bias still remain and here [in sociology], as elsewhere, they bar the way to science. It displeases man to renounce the unlimited power over the social order he has so long attributed to himself; and on the other hand, it seems to him that, if collective forces really exist, he is necessarily obliged to submit to them without being able to modify them. This makes him inclined to deny their existence. In vain have repeated experiences taught him that this omnipotence, the illusion of which he complacently entertains, has always been a cause of weakness in him; that his power over things really began only when he recognized that they have a nature of their own, and resigned himself to learning this nature from them. Rejected by all other sciences, this deplorable prejudice stubbornly maintains itself in sociology. Nothing is more urgent than to liberate our science from it, and this is the principal purpose of our efforts,"—Emile Durkheim (1938: lviii)

". . . it appears like a grandiose dream to think of controlling according to the will of man the course of social evolution. . ."
—Wm. F. Ogburn (1922:346)

The belief that man controls his civilization is widespread and deeply rooted. Customs and institutions, tools and machines, science, art, and philosophy are but man's creations and are therefore here only to do

*Reprinted with the permission of Farrar, Straus & Giroux, Inc., from *The Science of Culture* by Leslie A. White, copyright © 1949, 1969 by Leslie A. White.

Professor White, who taught at the University of Michigan for more than thirty years, is currently research anthropologist at the University of California at Santa Barbara.

his bidding. It lies within man's power, therefore, to chart his course as he pleases, to mold civilization to his desires and needs. At least so he fondly believes.

Thus we find a distinguished British scientist, the late Sir James Jeans, assuring us that:

> We no longer believe that human destiny is a plaything for spirits, good and evil, or for the machinations of the Devil. There is nothing to prevent our making the earth a paradise again—except ourselves. The scientific age has dawned, and we recognize that man himself is the master of his fate, the captain of his soul. He controls the course of his ship, and so, of course, is free to navigate it into fair waters or foul, or even to run it on the rocks (Jeans 1931:109).

Mr. Stanley Field, President of the Field Museum (now the Chicago Natural History Museum), appeals to anthropologists in espousing Free Will:

> But if we listen to the anthropologists, who can scientifically demonstrate that it is not color of skin, or type of hair or features, or difference of religion, that creates problems between peoples, but factors for which man is responsible and which he can control or change if he will, then we shall at least come within sight of that better world which we now realize we must achieve if we are not finally to perish as victims of our own perversity (Field 1943:9).

Professor Lewis G. Westgate, in an article in Scientific Monthly, tells us that man can "take the problem of his future in hand and solve it":

> The mind that can weigh the infinitely distant stars . . . track down the minute carriers of disease . . . dig the Panama Canal . . . can solve its social problems when and if it decides to do so (Westgate 1943: 165).

It would thus seem that the salvation of an earlier era has become the social reconstruction of today: we can achieve it if we will; if we fail it is because of our "perversity."

Father Wilhelm Schmidt, the leader of the *Kulturkreis* school of ethnology, and his disciples in America believe firmly in free will; indeed, it appears to be one of their cardinal principles (Schmidt 1939:8; Sieber and Mueller 1941:119-120). And even V. Gordon Childe, whose work is for the most part infused with the spirit of scientific materialism and determinism, says, in a book significantly entitled *Man Makes Himself*, that "changes in culture . . . can be initiated, controlled, or delayed by the conscious and deliberate choice of their human authors and executors" (Childe 1936:19).

When, however, we look for examples of man's control over culture we begin first to wonder, then to doubt. We will not begin our inquiry by asking if two World Wars in one generation are evidence of planning or perversity, or whether Germany and Japan were crushed and Soviet Russia made dominant in Eurasia in accordance with a farsighted plan or as a result of blindness and folly. We will start with something much more modest. During the last century we have witnessed attempts to control tiny and relatively insignificant segments of our culture, such as spelling, the calendar, the system of weights and measures, to name but a few. There have been repeated and heroic attempts to simplify spelling and make it more rational, to devise a more rational calendar, and to adopt an ordered system of weights and measures instead of the cumbersome, illogical agglomeration of folk measurements we now use. But what successes can we point to? Reform in spelling has been negligible. We have succeeded to a considerable extent but not wholly in eliminating the *u* from such words as *honor*. But to do away with silent letters, such as the *b* in *lamb*, is too big a mountain for us to move. And such spellings and pronunciations as *rough, cough, dough,* and *through* are much too strong to yield to our puny efforts. It usually takes a great political and social upheaval to effect a significant change in spellings or a calendrical system as the French and Bolshevik revolutions have made clear. And as for the metric system, it has found a place among the little band of esoterics in science, but yards, ounces, rods, pints, and furlongs still serve—awkwardly and inefficiently—the layman.

We begin to wonder. If we are not able to perform such tiny and insignificant feats as eliminating the *b* from *lamb*, or modifying our calendar system, how can we hope to construct a new social order on a worldwide scale?

Let us look about us further. Men and women are forever contending with fashions. Man perennially rebels against his attire. It is often uncomfortable, injurious to the health at times, and, some men think, the ordinary costume is unesthetic, the formal attire ridiculous. But what can he do? He must wear his coat and tie no matter how hot the weather. He is not permitted to wear pink or blue shoes. And as for "evening clothes"—he must submit to them or stay home. Man's vaunted control over civilization is not particularly conspicuous in this sector.

But if man is helpless, woman is an abject slave, in the grip of fashion. She must submit to any change, no matter how fantastic or ugly. To be sure, she may not realize that the new designs are fantastic and ugly at the time; "the latest style" can becloud a woman's judgment. But one has only to browse through an album of old snapshots to realize that beauty, grace, and charm do not dominate the course of fashion.

And as for women's skirts! First they are short; then they are long. A distinguished anthropologist, Professor A. L. Kroeber of the University of California, has made a very interesting and revealing study of the dimensions of women's dresses over a considerable period of time. He found that "the basic dimensions of modern European feminine dress alternate with fair regularity between maxima and minima which in most cases average about fifty years apart so that the full-wave length of their periodicity is around a century" (Kroeber and Richardson 1940: 148; Kroeber 1919). The rhythms are regular and uniform. Women have nothing to say about it. Even the designers and creators must conform to the curve of change. We find no control by man—or woman—here, only an inexorable and impersonal trend. When a maximum point on the curve is reached, the trend is reversed and skirts lengthen or shorten as the case may be. Women are helpless; they can do nothing but follow the trend. When the curve ascends they must shorten their dresses; when it descends, they must lengthen them. It may seem remarkable that a great class of citizens who cannot even control the dimensions of their own skirts will nevertheless organize themselves into clubs, to administer the affairs of the world. We shall return to this point later.

Few men would undertake to repair an automobile or a radio without some understanding of its mechanism. We tend more and more nowadays to leave medicine and surgery to those who know. Knowledge and skill are required even to make good pies or home brew. But in matters of society and culture everyone feels qualified to analyze, diagnose, and prescribe. It is one of the premises of democracy that not only do the people rule, but they have the requisite knowledge and understanding to do it effectively. In matters political, one man's view is as good as another's.

When, however, we examine the knowledge and understanding with which the affairs of the nation are administered we begin again to wonder. We find the most august authorities espousing different and even contradictory views on such subjects as inflation, the function of labor leaders, the divorce rate, the popularity of crooners, and so on. This is a picture of the anarchy of ignorance, not of wisdom.

When we turn from matters of national proportions, such as the cause of inflation, to lesser problems we are not always reassured. Does capital punishment diminish the number of murders? Does the use of alcohol affect the divorce rate? Why do people keep dogs? They are noisy, dirty, unhealthful, useless, and expensive. To say that they are kept because people like them is merely to phrase the problem in a different form. Why don't they "like" raccoons? They are cute, clean in their habits, and very amiable.

The fact is, we don't really know very much about the civilization we live in. Let us take one of the simplest and most elementary questions imaginable: Why does our society prohibit polygamy? Other societies permit plural mates, and Western Europe once did, also. But now we feel very strongly about it. We will put a man in a prison for years if he takes unto himself more than one wife at one time. His wives may be perfectly satisfied with the arrangement and he may have injured no one. Yet we put him in gaol.[1] Why? Why not have one more wife and one less schoolmarm?

There are, to be sure, ready answers to these questions: polygamy is "wrong," "immoral," "undemocratic," etc. But practices are not prohibited because they are "wrong"; they are wrong because they have been prohibited. It is not wrong to buy and sell whiskey now; it was while the Eighteenth Amendment was on the books. And as for democracy and equality, we permit a man to have two yachts if he can afford them, why not two wives?

I know of no really adequate answer to this question in such literature of social science as I am acquainted with. As a matter of fact, the question is very seldom raised. I have looked for it in a great number of treatises on sociology and anthropology written during the last quarter century without finding it. Some social scientists of the latter half of the nineteenth century tried to explain the prohibition of polygamy but we cannot accept their conclusions.

The fact is we are ignorant. We do not know the solution to such an elementary problem as singular or plural mates. And in our day, we have not reached the point of asking such questions, to say nothing of answering them. As Archibald McLeish has said, "We know all the answers, but we have not yet asked the questions." Over a half-century ago the great French savant, Emile Durkheim, commented upon the immaturity of social science as follows:

> In the present state of the science we really do not even know what are the principal social institutions, such as the state, or the family; what is the right of property or contract . . . We are almost completely ignorant of the factors on which they depend . . . ; we are scarcely beginning to shed even a glimmer of light on some of these points. Yet one has only to glance through the works on sociology to see how rare is the appreciation of this ignorance and these difficulties (Durkheim 1938: xlvi).

Despite the progress that has been made since *The Rules* was written, this statement has a certain relevance today. If the science of society and civilization is still so immature as to be unable to solve such tiny and elementary problems as the prohibition of polygamy, where are the knowledge and understanding requisite to planning a new social system, to constructing a new world order? One would not expect a savage craftsman, whose best tools are made of chipped flint, to design and build a locomotive.

Let us have a look at this civilization man thinks he controls. The first thing we notice is its antiquity. There is no part of it, whether it be technology, institutions, science or philosophy, that does not have its roots in the remote past. The lens of the new 200 inch telescope, for example, is made of glass. Glass emerged from the manufacture of faience in ancient Egypt, which in turn originated apparently as a by-product of burning bricks and pottery, which followed the use of sun-dried brick, and, earlier, mud daubs of Neolithic or even Paleolithic huts. The United Nations can be traced back to primitive tribal councils and beyond. Modern mathematics goes back to counting on one's fingers, and so on. Culture is as old as man himself. It had its beginnings a million odd years ago when man first started to use articulate speech, and it has continued and developed to the present day. Culture is a continuous, cumulative, and progressive affair.

Everyone—every individual, every generation, every group—has, since the very earliest period of human history, been born into a culture, a civilization, of some sort. It might be simple, crude and meager, or it might be highly developed. But all cultures, whatever their respective degrees of development, have technologies (tools, machines), social systems (customs, institutions), beliefs (lore, philosophy, science) and forms of art. This means that when a baby is born into a cultural milieu, he will be influenced by it. As a matter of fact, his culture will determine how he will think, feel, and act. It will determine what language he will speak, what clothes, if any, he will wear, what gods he will believe in, how he will marry, select and prepare his foods, treat the sick, and dispose of the dead. What else *could* one do but react to the culture that surrounds him from birth to death? No people makes its own culture; it inherits it ready-made from its ancestors or borrows it from its neighbors.

It is easy enough for man to believe that he has made his culture, each generation contributing its share, and that it is he who controls and directs its course through the ages. Does he not chip the arrowheads and stone axes, build carts and dynamos, coin money and spend it, elect presidents and depose kings, compose symphonies and carve statues, worship gods and wage war? But one cannot always rely upon the obvious. It was once obvious that the earth remained stationary while the sun moved; anyone could see that for himself. We are now approaching a point in modern thought where we are beginning to suspect that it is not man who controls culture but the other way around. The feat of Copernicus in dispelling the geocentric illusion over four hundred years ago is being duplicated in our day by the culturologist who is dissipating the anthropocentric illusion that man controls his culture.

Although it is man who chips arrowheads, composes symphonies, etc., we cannot explain culture merely by saying that "man produced it." There is not a single question that we would want to ask about culture that can be answered by saying "Man did thus and so." We want to know why culture developed as it did; why it assumed a great variety of forms while preserving at the same time a certain uniformity, why the rate of cultural change has accelerated. We want to know why some cultures have money and slaves while others do not; why some have trial by jury, others ordeal by magic; why some have kings, others chiefs or presidents; why some use milk, others loathe it; why some permit, others prohibit, polygamy. To explain all these things by saying, "Man wanted them that way" is of course absurd. A device that explains everything explains nothing.

Before we go very far we discover that we must disregard man entirely in our efforts to explain cultural growth and cultural differences—in short, culture or civilization as a whole. Man may be regarded as a constant so far as cultural change is concerned. Man is one species and, despite differences of skin, eye, and hair color, shape of head, lips, and nose, stature, etc., which after all are superficial, he is highly uniform in such fundamental features as brain, bone, muscle, glands, and sense organs. And he has undergone no appreciable evolutionary change during the last 50,000 years at least. We may, therefore, regard man as a constant both with regard to the races extant today, and with regard to his ancestors during the last tens of thousands of years. Man has a certain structure and certain functions; he has certain desires and needs. These are related to culture, of course, but only in a *general*, not a specific, way. We may say that culture as a whole serves the needs of man as a species. But this does not and cannot help us at all when we try to account for the variations of specific cultures. You cannot explain variables by appeal to a constant. You cannot explain the vast range of cultural variation by invoking man, a biological constant. In England in A. D. 1500 there was one type of culture; in Japan, another. Neither culture can be explained in terms of the physical type associated with it. Culture underwent change in England between A.D. 1500 and 1900, as it did in Japan. But these changes cannot be explained by pointing to the inhabitants in each case; they did not change. Plainly, we cannot explain cultures in terms of Man.

Nor can cultural differences be explained in terms of environment. Quite apart from the difficulty of accounting for differences in musical styles, forms of writing, codes of etiquette, rules of marriage, mortuary rites, etc., in terms of environment, we soon discover that even economic, industrial, and social systems cannot be so explained. The environment of Central Europe so far as climate, flora, fauna, topography, and mineral resources are concerned has remained constant for centuries. The culture of the region, however, has varied enormously. Here again we see the fallacy of explaining the variable by appeal to a constant.

If, then, we cannot explain cultures in terms of race or physical type, or in terms of psychological processes, and if appeal to environment is equally futile, how *are* they to be accounted for and made intelligible to us?

There seems to be only one answer left and that is fairly plain—after one becomes used to it, at least. Cultures must be explained in terms of culture. As we have already noted, culture is a continuum. Each trait or organization of traits, each stage of development, grows out of an earlier cultural situation. The steam engine can be traced back to the origins of metallurgy and fire. International cartels have grown out of all the processes of exchange and distribution since the Old Stone Age and before. Our science, philosphy, religion, and art have developed out of earlier forms. Culture is a vast stream of tools, utensils, customs, beliefs that are constantly interacting with each other, creating new combinations and syntheses. New elements are added constantly to the stream; obsolete traits drop out. The culture of today is but the cross section of this stream at the present moment, the resultant of the age-old process of interaction, selection, rejection, and accumulation that has preceded us. And the culture of tomorrow will be but the culture of today plus one more day's growth. The numerical coefficient of today's culture may be said to be 365,000,000 (i.e., a million years of days); that of tomorrow: 365,000,000 + 1. The culture of the present was determined by the past and the culture of the future will be but a continuation of the trend of the present. Thus, in a very real sense *culture makes itself*. At least, if one wishes to explain culture scientifically, he must proceed *as if* culture made itself, *as if* man had nothing to do with the determination of its course or content. Man must *be* there, of course, to make the existence of the culture process possible. But the nature and behavior of the process itself is self-determined. It rests upon its own principles; it is governed by its own laws.

Thus, culture makes man what he is and at the same time makes itself. An Eskimo, Bantu, Tibetan, Swede, or American is what he is, thinks, feels, and acts as he does, because his culture influences—"stimulates"—him in such a way as to evoke these responses. The Eskimo or American has had no part in producing the culture into which he was thrust at birth. It was already there; he could not escape it; he could do nothing but react to it, and that on its own terms. The English language, the Christian religion, our political institutions, our mills, mines, factories, railroads, telephones, armies, navies, race tracks, dance halls, and all the other thousands of things that comprise our civilization are here in existence today. They have weight, mass, and momentum. They cannot be made to disappear by waving a wand, nor can their structure and behavior be altered by an act of will. We must come to terms with them as we find them today. And they will be tomorrow what their trend of development in the past dictates. We can only trot along with them, hoping to keep up.

Man has long cherished the illusion of omnipotence. It is flattering and comforting to his ego. In days gone by, man has believed that he could control the weather; countless primitive peoples have had rituals for making rain, stilling high winds, or averting storms. Many have had ceremonies by means of which the course of the sun in the heavens could be "controlled." With the advance of science, however, man's faith in his omnipotence has diminished. But he still believes that he can control his civilization.

The philosophy of science—of cause and effect relationships, of determinism—has been firmly established in the study of physical phenomena. It is well entrenched in the biological field, also. Psychology may have demonstrated the operation of the principles of cause and effect, of determinism, in mental processes, and may have dispelled the notion of free will for the *individual*. But social science is still so immature as to permit one to find refuge in a collective free will. As Professor A. L. Kroeber has recently observed:

> I suspect that the resistance [to the thesis of cultural determinism] goes back to the common and deeply implanted assumption that our wills are free. As this assumption has had to yield ground elsewhere, it has taken refuge in the collective, social, and historical sphere. Since the chemists, physiologists, and psychologists have unlimbered their artillery, the personal freedom of the will is thankless terrain to maintain. Culture they have not yet attacked; so that becomes a refuge. Whatever the degree to which we have ceased to assert being free agents as individuals, in the social realm we can still claim to shape our destinies. The theologian is piping pretty small, but the social reformer very loud. We are renouncing the kingdom of heaven, but going to establish a near-millenium on earth. Our personal wills may be determined, but by collectivizing them we can still have social freedom (Kroeber and Richardson 1940:152).

Primitive man could believe that he could control the weather only because he was ignorant; he knew virtually nothing of meteorology. And today, it is only our profound and comprehensive ignorance of the nature of culture that makes it possible for us to believe that we direct and control it. As man's knowledge and understanding grew in meteorology, his illusion of power and control dissipated. And as our understanding of culture increases, our illusion of control will languish and disappear. As Durkheim once observed, "as far as social facts are concerned, we still have the mentality of primitives" (Durkheim 1915:27).

Needless to say, this is not the view taken by many today who look to science for our salvation. Far from expecting belief in our ability to control to diminish with the advance of social science, many people expect just the reverse. It has become the fashion these days to declare that if only our social sciences were as advanced as the physical sciences, then we could control our culture as we now control the physical forces of nature. The following quotation from a letter published in *Science* recently is a conservative statement of this point of view:

For if, by employing the scientific method, men can come to understand and control the atom, there is reasonable likelihood that they can in the same way learn to understand and control human group behavior . . . It is quite within reasonable probability. that social science can provide these techniques [i.e., for "keeping the peace"] if it is given anything like the amount of support afforded to physical science in developing the atomic bomb (Bassett 1946:25-26).

In similar vein Professor Gordon W. Allport of Harvard observes that "the United States spent two billion dollars on the invention of the atomic bomb" and asks "What is there absurd in spending an equivalent sum, if necessary, on the discovery of means for its control?" (Allport 1947:23).

The premise underlying this view is unsound. It assumes that wars are caused, or at least made possible, by ignorance and the lack of social control that goes with ignorance. It assumes that, given understanding through generous grants of funds to social scientists, wars could be prevented—the "peace could be kept." The lack of understanding and realism displayed here is pathetic. The instinct of self-preservation of a society that subsidized atom bomb inventors rather than social scientists holding views such as these is a sure one. Wars are not caused by ignorance, nor can "the peace be kept" by the findings of social scientists. Wars are struggles between social organisms—called *nations*—for survival, struggles for the possession and use of the resources of the earth, for fertile fields; coal, oil, and iron deposits; for uranium mines; for seaports and waterways; for markets and trade routes; for military bases. No amount of understanding will alter or remove the *basis* of this struggle, any more than an understanding of the ocean's tides will diminish or terminate their flow.

But the fallacy of assuming that we can increase and perfect our control over civilization through social science is even more egregious than we have indicated. To call upon science, the essence of which is acceptance of the principles of cause and effect and determinism, to support a philosophy of Free Will, is fairly close to the height of absurdity. Verily, Science has become the modern magic! The belief that man can work his will upon nature and man alike *if only he had the right formulas* once flourished in primitive society as *magic*. It is still with us today, but we now call it Science.

No amount of development of the social sciences would increase or perfect man's control over civilization by one iota. In the man-culture system, man is the dependent, culture the independent, variable. What man thinks, feels, and does is determined by his culture. And culture behaves in accordance with its own laws. A mature development of social science would only make this fact clear.

The philosophy of Free Will and omnipotence is rampant in the field of education (see p. 107 [of White 1949]). "Educators," high school principals, commencement orators, and others never seem to tire of telling the world that its salvation lies in education. An eminent anthropologist, the late Clark Wissler, looking at our civilization as he would at other cultures of mankind—of the Blackfoot Indians, the Bantu tribes of Africa, or the aborigines of Australia—finds that a faith in education and its efficacy to cure all ills is a characteristic trait of our culture. "The fact is," he says, "that we seek to solve every difficulty by education. . . . No matter what it may be, the combating of disease, the inauguration of a new public service, the appreciation of art, dress reform, or anything of that kind, we look to education to make it universal and popular." Our faith in education has, in fact, become our religion, as Dr. Wissler sees it:

"Our culture is characterized by an overruling belief in something we call education—a kind of mechanism to propitiate the intent of nature in the manifestation of culture. Our implicit faith that this formula, or method, will cause this purpose to be more happily fulfilled, is our real religion" (Wissler 1923:8).

Dr. Wissler compares our education formula with the magical formulas of primitive tribes:

> We often find among peoples we choose to call less civilized, a class of men whom we designate as shamans, medicine men, conjurors, etc. . . . Where such men flourish they are called upon whenever the course of events goes wrong, sickness, famine, love, war, no matter what the nature of the trouble may be, and they always proceed in one way: i.e., recite or demonstrate a formula of some kind. They may sing it, they may dance it, or they may merely act it out—no matter, the idea is that if you go through with the correct formula the forces of nature will right the wrong. . . . In every culture formulae are used to propitiate nature in whatever form of gods or powers she is conceived, and . . . cultures differ not in this, for so far they are all alike, but as to the kinds of formulae into which they put their faith. Our great formula for bringing about the realization of our lead-

ing ideals is education. . . . It is a kind of grand over-formula by which we hope to perpetuate and perfect our culture . . . (Wissler 1923:8-10).

The faith of primitive man in his formulas and rituals, his medicine men and conjurors, was not shaken by a perpetual repetition of the ills they were supposed to prevent or cure. Lack of success did not prove to him that his formulas and rituals were inefficacious; it only convinced him that he needed more and better magic. And we who look to education for our "salvation" are not shaken in our faith by the spectacle of tragedy piled upon disaster. What we need, we say, is more education.

To primitive man, magic was a means, available to mankind, to exert influence over the external world and so to shape it to his needs and desires. We think of education as an instrument with which we can transform society and mould it to our will. But education is not a force or instrument *outside* of society, but a *process within it*. It is, so to speak, a physiologic process of the social organism. Education is a means employed by society in carrying on its own activities, in striving for its own objectives. Thus, during peacetime, society educates for peace, but when the nation is at war, it educates for war. In times of peace, munitions-makers are "Merchants of Death"; in wartime, "Victory is Their Business." In peacetime, He is the Prince of Peace, but when war comes it's "Praise the Lord and pass the ammunition." It is not people who control their culture through education; it is rather the other way around: education, formal and informal, is the process of bringing each new generation under the control of a system of culture. It is unrealistic in the extreme, therefore, to think of education reforming society from the outside. No one has stated the relationship between education and society better than the great French social scientist, Emile Durkheim:

But this is to attribute to education a power which it does not possess. It is only the image, the reflection of society. Education imitates society and reproduces it in abridged form, but it does not create it. Education is healthy when the nation itself is in a healthy state, but, not having the power of self modification, it becomes corrupted when the nation decays. If the moral milieu as it is experienced by the teachers themselves is corrupt, they cannot fail to be affected by it; how then can they impress upon those whom they train an outlook that differs from the one that

they have received? Each generation is brought up by the previous generation and it is necessary therefore to reform the latter
if it is to improve the one which follows it. We go around in cir-
cles. At long intervals it may well happen that someone may
come along whose ideas and aspirations are in advance of those
of his contemporaries, but the moral constitution of a people is
not made over by these isolated individuals. No doubt it pleases
us to believe that one eloquent voice is sufficient to transform the
social fabric as if by magic, but, here as elsewhere, something is
not produced from nothing. The strongest wills cannot create
out of nothing forces which do not exist, and failures in experience always come to dispel these easy illusions. Besides, even
though a pedagogical system could succeed by an incomprehen-
sible miracle in establishing itself in antagonism to the social
system, it would have no effect by reason of this very antagonism.
If the collective organization (society) is maintained from which
the moral state that one wishes to combat is derived, then the
child cannot fail to be influenced by it from the moment he
comes into contact with it. The artificial milieu of the school
can only protect him for a time and then but feebly. In proportion as the real world takes greater hold of him, it will destroy the
work of the educator. Thus education cannot reform itself unless
society itself is reformed. And in order to do that we must go to
the causes of the malady from which it suffers (Durkheim 1897:
427-28).

The position taken here will of course be vigorously denied and opposed. People do not give up their illusions easily. A. L. Kroeber said:

Our minds instinctively resist the first shock of the recognition
of a thing [cultural determinism] so intimately woven into us
and yet so far above and so uncontrollable by our wills. We feel
driven to deny its reality, to deny even the validity of dealing with
it as an entity; just as men at large have long and bitterly resented
admitting the existence of purely automatic forces and system in
the realm that underlies and carries and makes possible the existence of our personalities: the realm of nature (Kroeber 1919:
263).

A common reaction—verbal reflex—to the theory of cultural determinism is to brand it "fatalistic" or "defeatist." Long ago William

James branded as "the most pernicious and immoral of fatalisms" the philosophy of "the contemporary sociological school" that espoused "general laws and predetermined tendencies," and "denied the vital importance of individual initiative" and Free Will ("I believe in free-will myself," he says. (James 1890: 2439; 1880:442)). And today another student of philosophy, Dr. David Bidney, writing in the American Anthropologist, has repeatedly called the deterministic point of view of culturology "fatalistic." The choice of words is significant. Why is it that when one employs the principle of cause and effect in the realm of physical and chemical phenomena no one cries "fatalism," but the instant one applies it to human cultural phenomena this accusation leaps forth? Why is it that an admission of our inability to control the weather brings forth no charge of "defeatism" whereas this reproach is promptly levelled against anyone who recognizes man's inability to control the course of civilization?

The reason is fairly plain. "Fatalism" implies Free Will; "defeatism," omnipotence. When atoms, cells, or tissues behave in accordance with their nature and properties no one calls it fatalistic because no one expects freedom of choice and action of them. But when one asserts that cultural phenomena have a nature of their own and consequently must behave in terms of their nature, the response is not an acceptance of the principle of cause and effect but a charge of "fatalism." "To many educated minds," the great English anthropologist, E. B. Tylor, wrote many years ago, "there seems something presumptuous and repulsive in the view that the history of mankind is part and parcel of the history of nature, that our thoughts, wills, and actions accord with laws as definite as those which govern the motion of the waves, the combination of acids and bases, and the growth of plants. . . If law is anywhere it is everywhere" (Tylor 1871: 2, 24). We have combined "a scientific realism, based on mechanism," says Alfred North Whitehead, with "an unwavering belief in the world of men and of the higher animals as being composed of *self-determining organisms*" (Whitehead 1933:94; emphasis ours). He feels that this "radical inconsistency" is responsible for "much that is half-hearted and wavering in our civilization. It . . . enfeebles . . . [thought] by reason of the inconsistency lurking in the background."

Implicit in the charge of "fatalism" and "defeatism" is the further notion of refutation. To brand a view "fatalistic" is, to many minds, to call it false as well. "Cultural determinism is fatalistic and therefore false," is about the way the reasoning would go if it were made explicit. *"How can determinism possibly exist?"* is the question that is implied but unspoken. "Determinism is unthinkable." And so it is to one possessed by a philosophy of free will.[2] We find this point of view rather well expressed by Lawrence K. Frank in a recent article, "What is Social Order?"

> Perhaps the major obstacle we face today, therefore, is this essentially defeatist tradition expressed in the various conceptions of social order described earlier, as above and beyond all human control . . . In this situation, therefore, we can and we must find the courage to view social order as that which must be achieved by man himself (Frank 1944:475).

Of course man can "find the courage" to view social order as something "that must be achieved by himself." It does not take courage to do this, however; what is required is ignorance and hope. "Must find the courage," "must be achieved by man himself," is hardly the language of science. It is, rather, exhortation and rhetoric—of a type with which we have long been familiar: "if we will but purpose in our hearts . . ."

No doubt the first to question man's control over the weather, the first to claim that the winds will blow, the rain and snow fall, the seasons come and go, in accordance with their own nature rather than in obedience to man's wish and will expressed in spell and ritual, were accused of "fatalism"and "defeatism," if, indeed, they were not dealt with more harshly. But, in time, we have come to accept our impotence in this regard and to become reconciled to it. If it be argued that man cannot control the weather because that is a part of the external world whereas culture, being man-made, is subject to his control, it must be pointed out that the exact opposite is the case. It is precisely in the realm of the external world that man's control is possible. He can harness the energies of rivers, fuels, and atoms because he, as one of the forces of nature, lies *outside* their respective systems and can therefore act upon them. But man, as an animal organism, as a species, lies *within* the man-culture system, and there he is the dependent, not the independent, variable; his behavior is merely the function of his culture, not its determinant. Both theoretically and practically, therefore, it is possible for man to exert more control over the weather than over culture, for he can exert *some* control over the former even now and he may increase this control in the future. But he exerts no control whatever over his culture and theoretically there is no possibility of his ever doing so.

The usual reactions to this manifesto of cultural determinism are as unwarranted as are the assumptions of Free Will, from which, of course, these responses flow. After expostulating on the theme of "fatalism" and "defeatism" the conventional protest goes on to demand, "What is the use then of our efforts? Why should we try to do anything to improve our lot if we have no control over our culture? Why not just sit back and let the evolutionary process take care of everything? Of what use could a science of culture possibly be to us if control lies beyond our grasp? What good is an understanding of culture if there is nothing we can do about it?"

These questions are naive and betray a lack of understanding of what the cultural deteminist—the culturologist—is trying to say. The determinist does not assert that man is irrelevant to the culture process. He knows full well that the contrary is the case; that man is an absolute prerequisite to it, that without man there could be no culture. He realizes very clearly the essential role that man plays in the system that is man-and-culture. What the culturologist contends is that in this system the human organism is not the determinant; that the behavior of the culture process cannot be explained in terms of this organism but only in terms of the culture itself; that the growth and changes among the Indo-European languages, for example, cannot be accounted for in terms of man's nerves, muscles, senses, or organs of speech; or in terms of his hopes, needs, fears, or imagination. Language must be explained in terms of language.

But to turn to some of the specific questions with which dissatisfaction with the philosophy of determinism is expressed. In the first place, we cannot "just sit back" and let the evolutionary process take care of all of our problems. While we live we are confronted by our culture and we must come to terms with it. Even just sitting back, incubating a case of dementia praecox, is "doing something about it." So is committing suicide; as a matter of fact, suicide rates for various societies provide excellent indexes of cultural determinism. In some societies the rate is high; in others suicide is virtually non-existent. This is not because suicide determinants are more abundant in the chromosomes of some populations than of others. It is due to the fact that the cultural determinants vary: hara-kiri is something that a culture does to an organism that, of its own nature, tends to persevere in that form of motion we call "Life." It is obvious that we cannot avoid reacting to our culture.

To assume that the process of cultural evolution will take care of everything without effort on our part is of course absurd, and constitutes no part of the determinist's philosophy. Of course we must exert ourselves while we live; we cannot do otherwise. But the question is not "Who does the work, ourselves or cultural evolution?" It is obvious that the energy is expended by or through human beings. The question is, *What determines the nature, the form and content of this expression of energy in the culture process, the human organism or the extra-somatic culture?* The answer is of course fairly obvious—after a small amount of reflection. Let us consider two groups of human organisms, A and B. Group A raises taro, catches fish, carves wood, makes no pottery, speaks a Polynesian language, has chiefs but no currency, is non-literate, drinks kava, is greatly concerned with genealogy, and so on. Group B mines coal and iron, talks Welsh, imports its food from the outside, uses money, is literate, drinks ale, etc. Now the question is, Why does each group behave as it does? Is it that one group of organisms possesses traits or characteristics—genes, instincts, or psychological tendencies—that cause them to drink kava rather than ale? This is, of course, ridiculous; the one group of organisms is fundamentally like the other biologically. It is obvious that each group of organisms behaves as it does because each is reacting to a particular set of cultural stimuli. It is obvious also that a consideration of the human organism is totally irrelevant to the question. Why is one group stimulated by one set of stimuli rather than by another? This is a cultural historical question, not a biological or psychological one. So, one is not so silly as to say, "Why should we mine coal or catch fish?Let our culture do it." The question is not who mines the coal, but what is the determinant of this behavior? And, the culturologist points out the obvious: the culture is the determinant.

The reaction of many sincere, altruistic and conscientious people, upon being told that it is not they who control their culture and direct its course, is "Why then should we try to do good, to better our lot and that of mankind?" We have answered this question in part already. In the first place one cannot avoid trying to do something. As long as one accepts life and is willing to continue with it he must exert himself. "Trying" is merely the name we give to the effort exerted in the process of living. To strive for this or that, therefore, is inseparable from our lives. But *what* one strives for and *how* his effort is expressed is determined by his culture. For example, the goal of one people may be eternal life in heaven for which their terrestrial existence is but a preparation. The goal of another might be the good life "here below." One group may deny the reality of sickness; another may admit its existence and try to combat it. One group may use charms and incantations; another, clinics and laboratories. Whatever the goal and whatever the means employed to reach it, is a matter determined by the culture of the group.

But, it should be pointed out with emphasis, this is not a philosophy of defeatism or hopelessness by any means. Least of all does it declare that one's efforts do not count. The fact that one's efforts to stamp out tuberculosis are culturally determined in no way minimizes the effort or the result. A life saved is a life saved. A letter written to a congressman has an *effect,* too, no matter what kind or how much. A resolution on world affairs passed by a woman's club has a real function in society, although it may be a very different one from that imagined by the good ladies. The question we raise is *not* one of the value of the effort or whether effort has consequences. Human effort is just as real as anything in the realm of the geologist. And effort is followed by consequences just as effect follows cause in physics and geology. Living human beings cannot help but exert themselves, and everything they do counts for something in one way or another. Far from wishing to deny or ignore this, we wish to emphasize it. But this is not the question raised by the culturologist, the cultural determinist. What he claims is, not that it is futile to try because what one does counts for nought, but that what one does, how he does it, and the end and purpose for which it is done is culturally determined, is determined by the culture of the group rather than by the free will of the individual or of the group. More than that, what a person or group desires is determined or at least defined by the culture, not by them. What constitutes the "good life" for any people is always culturally defined.

From the cultural determinist's point of view, human beings are merely the instruments through which cultures express themselves. A physician, saving lives each day, is an instrument through which certain cultural forces express themselves; if they were not there, or if they were different, the organism in question would not be practicing medicine or he would practice it in a different way. The gangster, evangelist, revolutionist, reformer, policeman, impoverished beggar, wealthy parasite, teacher, soldier, and shaman are likewise instruments of cultural action and expression; each is a type of primate organism grasped and wielded by a certain set of culture traits. It is only the inveterate habit of thinking anthropocentrically that makes this point of view strange or ridiculous.

But, granting that what we do counts even though it is culturally determined, of what use is it to develop a science of culture if we cannot control civilization or direct its course? We have a science of pathology in order to combat disease, sciences of physics and chemistry to control the external world. But if we do not control our culture and cannot ever hope to control it, of what use would a science of culture be? We might begin our reply to this question by asking, of what value is it to know the temperature of a star a million light years away? Questions such as these betray a limited understanding of science. Science is not primarily a matter of control in the sense of harnessing rivers with hydroelectric plants or constructing uranium piles. Science is a means of adjustment; control is but one aspect of adjustment. Man finds himself in a universe to which he must adjust if he is to continue to live in it. Mythology and science are means of adjustment; they are interpretations of the world in terms of which man behaves. There is, of course, a vast difference in terms of adjustment between a philosophy that interprets stars as a flock of snow birds lost in the sky, and one that measures their masses, distances, dimensions, and temperatures. This difference is a very practical one, too, in terms of the contribution that each philosophy makes to the security of life.

Our ancestors once thought they could control the weather as contemporary savages still do. They finally outgrew this illusion, even going so far as to outgrow calling the new view "fatalistic" and "defeatist." But we do not think a knowledge and an understanding of weather and climate useless. On the contrary, we are devoting more time and money to meteorology now than ever before. Here again we see the situation in terms of adjustment rather than *control*. We may not be able to control the weather but adjust to it we must. And knowledge and understanding make for more effective and satisfying adjustments. It would be advantageous if we *could* control the weather. But if we cannot, then weather prediction is the next best thing. And for prediction we must have knowledge and understanding.

So it is with culture. We cannot control its course but we can learn to predict it. As a matter of fact, we make predictions all the time and many of them are quite accurate: wheat production, traffic fatalities, freight car loadings, births, exhaustion of oil reserves, and many other matters are already within the reach of limited but nevertheless valuable prediction. If our ability to predict were greatly increased by the development and maturation of a science of culture the possibilities of a rational, effective, and humane adjustment between man and culture and between one cultural segment and another would be increased accordingly. If, for example, a science of culture could demonstrate that the trend of social evolution is toward larger political groupings, then the chances of making the futile attempt to restore or maintain the independence of small nations would be lessened. If the trend of cultural evolution is away from private property and free enterprise why strive to perpetuate them? If it could be shown that international wars will continue as long as independent, sovereign nations exist, them certain delusions now popular would find less nourishment and support. The fact is that culture has been evolving as an unconscious, blind, bloody, brutal, tropismatic process so far. It has not yet reached the point where intelligence, self-consciousness, and understanding are very conspicuous. Our ignorance is still deep-rooted and widespread. We do not understand even some of the elementary things—the prohibition of polygamy for example. In short, we are so ignorant that we can still believe that it is we who make our culture and control its course.

This ignorance is not surprising, however. It has not been very long since we gave up burning witches, cudgelling hysterics to drive out demons, and other savage practices. Even in technology, which tends to outstrip the social and ideological sectors, we have surpassed the savage at two points—fire-making and the use of the bow and arrow— only within the last century or two. Chemical matches are but a little more than a century old and the bow and arrow was used in bison hunting on the American plains in preference to the best firearms available at the time within the last hundred years. It is only yesterday, culturologically speaking, that a small portion of mankind began to emerge from a condition of savagery. For most of his career thus far man has subsisted wholly upon wild foods; less than two per cent of human history, as a matter of fact, has elapsed since the origin of agriculture. Other significant indexes: some 0.7 percent of culture history since the beginning of metallurgy, 0.35% since the first alphabet, 0.033% since Galileo, 0.009% since the publication of Darwin's *The Origin of Species*, and only 0.002% since William Jennings Bryan and the Scopes trial. A mature, urbane, and rational civilization is not to be achieved in a mere million years from the anthropoid level.

It should be made clear that if an adequate understanding should come about as a consequence of a science of culture it would not have been "us" who achieved it but our culture. In the interaction of elements in the culture process, those traits less effective in providing adequate adjustment in terms of understanding and control are gradually relinquished and replaced by more effective traits. Thus, bronze axes replace stone axes, ikons and spells give way to laboratories and clinics, and finally, a science of human culture begins to challenge the primitive philosophy of omnipotence and Free Will. The new science will of course have to prove its superiority over the older view just as astronomy, chemistry, and medicine have in other sectors of experience. The success of science—the philosophy of materialism, of cause and effect, of determinism—in the physical and biological sectors of experience encourages us greatly in the belief that this point of view and these techniques of interpretation will prove effective in the social sphere also.

Our role in this process is a modest one. Neither as groups nor as individuals do we have a choice of roles or of fates. Swedes are born into their culture just as Zulus, Tibetans, and Yankees are born into theirs. And each individual is thrust by birth into some particular place in the "magnetic field" of his culture, there to be molded by the particular organization of cultural influences that play upon him. Thus he may have the belief that typhoid exists only in the mind, or is caused by witches or bacilli, thrust upon him—or "into his mind." He may be endowed with a belief in personal immortality, the efficacy of prayer, or the Periodic Law of Mindeleyev. He may be inspired to preach the only true faith to the heathen in distant lands, or to wear out his life in a genetics laboratory, or to believe that "only saps work." To be sure, the response of the human organism to cultural stimulation will vary with the quality of the organism. Some will be silk purses; others, sows' ears. The order in which an organism undergoes experiences is important, too; the influence of events a, b, c, will not be the same as a, c, b. An experience will have one effect at fifteen; quite another at fifty. There is room, therefore, for almost infinite variety of permutation and combination in the experience of individual organisms.

Man discovers his place in the cosmos slowly and accepts it with extreme reluctance. Time was when his solid earth was planted in the center, the sun and stars spread upon the vault of heaven, and men and gods together acted out the drama of life and death. It was all so compact, so familiar, so secure. Then it was that man, like God, could cry "Let there be light" and there was light. Like God, too, man was "omnipotent," if, however, to a lesser degree. With his magic formulas, his spells, prayers, charms, and rituals, mighty man could control the weather, the seasons, and even enlist the gods in the service of man. Now it is different. Man finds himself but one of the innumerable animal species crawling about on an insignificant planetary speck, fighting, feeding, breeding, dying. Once the child of God, he now finds himself an ex-ape. But he has acquired a new faculty, one unknown among all other species: articulate speech. As a consequence of this, a new way of life has been developed: culture. But this culture, this mass of extra-somatic tools, institutions and philosophies, has a life and laws of its own. Man is just beginning to understand this.

Man is wholly at the mercy of external forces, astronomic and geologic. As a matter of fact, it is rather disconcerting to think of how narrow is the margin within which man lives. Change the temperature, velocity, amount of water, or atmosphere of the earth but a little and life would cease. It is a curious, and from a cosmic viewpoint, momentary, concatenation of circumstances that has made life possible. Man did long rebel against his dependence upon these outside forces; to be wholly at their mercy was unendurable. As a matter of fact, man has employed his precious and unique gift of speech more to deny the facts of his existence than to improve upon them. But a certain portion of the human race has come at last to accept our dependence upon nature and to try to make the most of it.

And so it is with culture. Belief in our omnipotence has, as Durkheim says, always been a source of weakness to us. But we are now discovering the true nature of culture and we can in time reconcile ourselves to this extra-somatic order as we have to the astronomic, geologic, and meteorologic orders. To give up magic and mythology which promised much but yielded nothing—nothing but the soothing comfort of illusion—was a painful experience. But to receive and accept a science and a technology which promises less but achieves a great deal is to reach a goal most men are loathe to lose. We may believe that knowledge and understanding of culture will make for a more satisfactory life just as these traits have been of value in physics and biology. To be sure, understanding culture will not, as we have argued here, alter its course or change the "fate" that it has in store for us, any more than understanding the weather or the tides will change them. But as long as man remains an inquiring primate he will crave understanding. And a growing Science of Culture will provide him with it.

NOTES

[1]We recall a recent instance in which a man was sent to the penitentiary for marrying some twelve women without ever bothering with the ritual of divorce. Had he been less honorable or chivalrous and lived with each woman without the formality of marriage, his "crime" would have been much less. This man served society well in a municipal railway system. His numerous wives pressed no complaint. Why did society feel it necessary to incarcerate him?

[2]Note that we have said *possessed by*, rather than "believe in." Philosophies possess, hold, animate, guide and direct the articulate, protoplasmic mechanisms that are men. Whether a man—an average man, typical of his group—"believes in" Christ or Buddha, Genesis or Geology, Determinism or Free Will, is not a matter of his own choosing. His philosophy is merely the response of his neuro-sensory-muscular-glandular system to the streams of cultural stimuli impinging upon him from the outside. What is called "philosophizing" is merely the interaction of these cultural elements within his organism. His "choice" of philosophic beliefs is merely a neurological expression of the superior strength of some of these extra-somatic cultural forces.

The following essay by John Copeland brings into focus many of the criticisms that have been levelled at Leslie White's culturology. Most of Copeland's specific comments concern White's "Man's Control Over Civilization" (cited in Copeland's essay as White 1949:330-359).

For additional critical comments on White, see Barnes (1960:xli-xlv), Harris (1968:634-653), Kardiner and Preble (1963:172-177), Service (1968a:405-406; and this volume), and Steward (1960).

White's reply to the critics of culturology is contained in his "Preface to the Second Edition" of The Science of Culture (1969). His earlier essay, "Culturological vs. Psychological Interpretations of Human Behavior" (1947; B-M, S-309), might also be consulted in conjunction with Copeland's critique.

One: 4

Culture and Man: Leslie A. White's Theses Re-examined

*John W. Copeland**

The theories propounded by Leslie A. White on the relationships between man and culture are worthy of serious attention; they are widely accepted but they have not received sufficiently detailed examination from the standpoint of the logic of scientific method.[1]

The theories in question are the following:

(A) Culture controls man. Man cannot control culture but can merely react to it. Culture is the independent variable, and the man the dependent variable.

(B) Men think that they choose the beliefs they have but this is an illusion.

Culture and Human Weakness

White's first claim of interest to us is that man does not and cannot control culture, or "exert any control over culture." Since White (1949: 139ff) defines culture as "an organization of phenomena—acts (patterns of behavior), objects (tools; things made with tools), ideas (belief, knowledge), and sentiments (attitudes, 'values')—that is dependent upon the use of symbols," his assertion that man cannot control culture can only mean that men cannot control their beliefs, customs, institutions, languages, tools, techniques, dwellings, or art forms.

The first type of evidence[2] which White (1949:332) offers in support of his theory is as follows:

*Reprinted with the permission of the author and publisher from *Southwestern Journal of Anthropology*, vol. 19, Spring 1963, pp. 109-120.

Formerly a student of anthropology, John W. Copeland is now professor of philosophy at Drew University.

During the last century we have witnessed attempts to control tiny and relatively insignificant segments of our culture, such as spelling, the calendar, the system of weights and measures, to name but a few. . . . But what successes can we point to? Reform in spelling has been negligible. . . . Such spellings-and-pronunciations as *rough, cough, dough,* and *through* are much too strong to yield to our puny efforts. It usually takes a great political and social upheaval to effect a significant change in spelling or a calendrical system as the French and Bolshevik revolutions have made clear. And as for the metric system, it has found a place among the little band of esoterics in science, but yards, ounces, rods, pints, and furlongs still serve . . . the layman.

There are two points concerning the meaning of the basic claim which should be mentioned immediately. First, White doe not restrict his claim here (or elsewhere) to the view that individuals cannot control their culture; he is saying that neither individuals *nor* groups can control culture. Secondly, as evidence for his claim that men have not succeeded in *controlling culture, White asserts that reforms have not been achieved; that except in cases of political and social upheaval, significant changes (reforms) generally do not occur. So that as evidence for the claim that men cannot control culture, White insists that significant planned changes* have not succeeded. Thus in denying that men can control culture, White is denying that they can change their culture in accordance with their plans. Does he mean by "control" something more than that? If there is any plus or surplus of meaning, I have been unable to detect it in White's writings; no definition of "control" is given. It is, of course, possible that when White says that men cannot control culture, he means that men in a given culture cannot have or manipulate cultural (e.g., technological or social) systems which are completely foreign to their experience. But since this is a virtual truism, it is difficult to believe that White would expend so much time and polemical energy fighting on its behalf. Again, it is possible that when White asserts that men cannot control culture he means that men cannot regulate its complete course; White repeatedly insists, following Durkheim, that man is not omnipotent and *therefore* he cannot control culture. But psychologists, sociologists, and theologians (White's main targets) have not, to my knowledge, ever said that man is omnipotent. Even the people whom White quotes as believing that science can save us, that science can enable us to remake the world to a considerable degree, did not say that man could change *everything* in the world. That man is not omnipotent is self-evident. But the claim that man cannot control culture unless he is omnipotent is not only not self-evident; there is no evidence for it at all. White's major thesis either rests on an arbitrary and elusive definition of "control" and is an empty tautology, or it is false, as we shall soon see.

The evidence which White does adduce in support of the theory that men cannot exert any control over culture is very indequate. There is, presumably, a reason why spelling habits are relatively slow changing. As White unwittingly acknowledges, these are "tiny and relatively insignificant segments of our culture." There are vastly more important matters which we believe need to be changed and progressively altered. In areas of real concern, reforms (significant planned changes) often occur. TVA and TWA are evidence that men have changed their techniques and tools in accordance with their plans, and thus, given White's definition, have changed their culture. Or consider planned changes in communications and in production techniques, such as the use of computers and the automation of factories. White does not mention these, for they would not help this case. Indeed, his examples are quite selective, not representative.

We need not draw counter-examples only from modern, industrialized societies. In Netherlands New Guinea, Awiitigaaj, in order to accomplish one of his other aims, planned to alter a basic institution of his village and he successfully accomplished both of his objectives. (I am indebted to Professor George P. Murdock for calling my attention to this case; see Pospisil 1958.)

An even more damaging criticism can be made of White's approach to this matter. Suppose large groups of scientists and scholars should come to believe that it is terribly important to the nation to change our system of weights and measures and even our spelling system. Convinced that reforms are badly needed, they would persuade Congress to have all government agencies use the metric system, a simplified spelling system, and the like. What would White say then? Would he still say that man cannot control culture? Since White (1949:350) asserts that man "exerts no control whatever over his culture and *theoretically* there is no possibility of his ever doing so" (italics mine), he would have to answer the previous question in the same old way. It is possible that White is using a private, idiosyncratic meaning of "theoretical," but to students of the logic of scientific method, his claim just cited means that it is *logically impossible* for man to exert any control over his culture. If this is what White means to assert, he holds his thesis as a dogma, not as an hypothesis. He assumes that there cannot be, in the nature of the case, *any* evidence against his claim; anything relevant could only count as evidence *for* it. The passage cited shows White would not give up his doctrine, no matter what the evidence might be. Consequently, an appeal to empirical evidence becomes irrelevant; White has removed the question from that domain.

But it is not necessary to base the claim that "White does not treat his thesis regarding man and culture as a scientific hypothesis" solely upon his assertion that it is theoretically impossible for men to control culture; the fact that a very important matter has been *omitted* from White's writings is also evidence for the criticism. Most students of the logic of scientific method maintain that for any empirical proposition to be cognitively meaningful, it must be possible to specify kinds of evidence which would confirm (or tend to confirm) the proposition, and it must also be possible to specify types of evidence which would disconfirm (or tend to disconfirm) the proposition in question. This does not mean that there must be evidence which in fact counts against the proposition; it means that one must be able to conceive or imagine states of affairs which would—*if* they occurred—tend to disconfirm the proposition. In reading White, one looks in vain for this evidence; the fact that no attempt is made to supply this type of information strengthens the claim that White does not present his basic thesis as a scientific hypothesis.

The second type of evidence which White (1949:350) uses in support of his view that man cannot control culture is as follows:

> [Man] can harness the energies of rivers, fuels, and atoms because he, as one of the forces of nature, lies *outside* their respective systems and can therefore act upon them. But man, as an animal organism, as a species, lies *within* the man-culture system, and there he is the dependent, not the independent, variable; his behavior is merely the function of his culture, not its determinant. Both theoretically and practically, therefore, it is possible for man to exert more control over the weather than over culture, for he can exert *some* control over the former even now and he may increase this control in the future. But he exerts no control whatever over his culture and theoretically there is no possibility of his ever doing so.

There are several defects in this passage employing the inside-outside analogy. First, the basic claim becomes an empty one. (A) When White insists that man is the dependent variable in the man-culture system, he is speaking of man as an animal organism, man minus status, role, or cultural experience of any kind. ("The formula for human behavior is:

Human organism x Cultural stimuli→Human behavior." White 1949: 18). Consequently, to say that unacculturated human organisms cannot exert any control over culture is to say nothing significant at all, since no one ever said that they could. (B) If the inside-outside analogy were sound, of course, it would enable White to justify the avoidance of empirical evidence: for the *a priori* contention that nothing within a system can succeed in altering the system would permit White to ignore the ways in which acculturated human beings change elements of their culture.

Secondly, there are two crucial inconsistencies within this passage which become clear once we draw out the implications of its assertions. (A) Just as human organisms devoid of cultural experience cannot exert any control over culture (an empty truism), so these same organisms obviously could not control weather, rivers, fuels, and atoms either. (B) *If* the fact that man is within the man-culture system were to prevent man from exerting control over his culture, it would follow that since culture is part of the man-culture system, culture could not control man either (despite White's emphatic assertion to the contrary). Indeed, how can White consistently say that man can control the *external* world, when man is part of the man-nature system? Thus White's inside-outside argument leads to a trivial conclusion and contains critical inconsistencies.

What White fails to see is that the *a priori* and dogmatic character of his claim that man cannot control culture makes any appeal to empirical evidence—whether to spelling habits, measuring systems, or fashions in dress—completely irrelevant. The "evidence" which White uses to support his thesis enables him to ignore much human behavior. Just as certain classical metaphysicians and scientists sat in their armchairs and insisted that they could thereby know truths about the world, so White takes the position that no matter *what* happens, no matter what men do, they cannot control culture. If some other theorist conducts or refers to actual empirical investigations which show that certain individuals or groups do make significant planned changes in belief systems, art forms, and/or other culture traits, White can ignore them, for his *a priori* doctrine tells him in advance that it is impossible for them to do so.

Explanations and Predictions

White's second claim of interest to us is that culture controls man, and therefore man can only react to culture. This point of view is expressed and explained in the following passage (White 1949:337):

> Everyone—every individual, every generation, every group—
> has, since the very earliest period of human history, been born
> into a culture, a civilization, of some sort. . . . All cultures,
> whatever their respective degrees of development, have technol-
> ogies (tools, machines), social systems (customs, institutions),
> beliefs (lore, philosophy, science), and forms of art. This means
> that when a baby is born into a cultural milieu, he will be in-
> fluenced by it. As a matter of fact, his culture will determine how
> he will think, feel, and act. It will determine what language he
> will speak, what clothes, if any, he will wear, what gods he will
> believe in, how he will marry, select and prepare his foods,
> treat the sick, and dispose of the dead. What else *could* one do
> but react to the culture that surrounds him from birth to death?[3]

As an illustration of the way in which culture controls us, White points
to the pressures upon human behavior of such cultural traits as fashions. With respect to the length of women's skirts, White (1949:333),
basing his claims upon Kroeber's well-known studies, asserts that
"women have nothing to say about it. Even the designers and creators
must conform to the curve of change. We find no control by man—or
woman—here, only an inexorable and impersonal trend." White (1949:
353-354) writes:

> From the cultural determinist's point of view, human be-
> ings are merely the instruments through which cultures express
> themselves. A physician, saving lives each day, is an instrument
> through which certain cultural forces express themselves. . . .
> The gangster, evangelist, revolutionist, reformer, policeman,
> impoverished beggar, wealthy parasite, teacher, soldier, and
> shaman are likewise instruments of cultural action and expres-
> sion; each is a type of primate organism grasped and wielded by
> a certain set of culture traits.

White's attempt to illustrate how his theory regards human beings
involves some serious difficulties. In the first place, for White to insist
that Ghandhi, Churchill, Hitler, and Mussolini were merely primate
organisms "grasped and wielded by a certain set of culture traits"
does not help us to explain why these individuals, rather than other
persons in the same cultural traditions, did what they did. It is one

thing to insist that an understanding of an individual requires that we know the traits of the culture in which he operates; it is quite another to assert that the behavior of the individual can be predicted and explained if (and only if) he is viewed as an instrument "grasped and wielded by a certain set of culture traits." The latter is, incidentally, picture-thinking.

Secondly, if White's claim that culture controls man *means* that the relation between culture and man is a one-way relation, that there is no interaction, that no individual or group ever influences culture traits, his theory oversimplifies the facts. The very attempt to buttress the thesis leads to counter-evidence quite readily. For example, White (1949:357) says that "Our role in this process is a modest one. Neither as groups nor as individuals do we have a choice of roles or of fates." White's claim, however, characterizes static societies far more than dynamic ones. For one of the cultural influences in, but not restricted to, American life is the value placed upon success, the rejection of the notion that each person has one and only one role or station in life and must "stay put," in favor of the notion of upward mobility, striving to escape from roles with which one is dissatisfied. And in fact individuals and groups do alter their positions; their deliberate strivings are successful in many cases. Indeed, they create new roles as well as alter old ones. This should indicate the causal interaction between culture and human behavior.[4]

White (1949:338) says that "There is not a single question that we would want to ask about culture that can be answered by saying 'Man did thus and so'." He adds that explanations of cultural practices which assert "Man wanted them that way" are absurd. Now there are two important points which need to be made concerning this claim. First, it assumes that there are two, and only two possibilities: either (A) *All* cultural practices can be explained by "Man wanted them that way," or (B) *No* cultural practices can be explained by "Man wanted them that way." But the proper reply is that while human wants are not the sole or total cause of particular events, they are often necessary conditions, significant causal factors required for the explanation and prediction of some events. The successful space flights of Titov, Gagarin, Glenn, and Carpenter could not have been predicted or explained in *complete independence* of the wants of these men and of a number of other men associated with their projects. At one point White (1949:353) says that his position does not deny that men want to do things and that their actions have consequences, but that what the cultural determinist insists upon is the *origin* of their purposes and goals, and these are to be found in the culture. But the impact of his position as White ordinarily expounds it is such as to deny that human wants can be causal factors. It is this emphasis that is mistaken; no disclaimer will hide or correct it.

The second point is that when White says that explanations in terms of human wants are absurd, and follows this claim with the assertion that "A device that explains everything explains nothing," his latter assertion is a damaging admission, since White constantly "explains" cultural practices by saying that culture did it, the culture was responsible.

On White's premises, how would we explain the writing of his own book, *The Science of Culture?* White (1949:356, 184) insists that "if an adequate understanding should come about as a consequence of a science of culture it would not have been 'us' who achieved it but our culture" and "It would be more realistic to say that his thinking and feeling are things that the culture *does* to the individual than to say that they are things that *he does.*" Given White's theory, on the title page of *The Science of Culture* in the place where the author's name usually appears, we should read "the culture wrote it." White was not the cause, or a part of the cause, of the appearance of the book; rather he was merely an instrument manipulated by cultural traits. No one ever did *anything*, on this theory.

Furthermore, it is inconsistent for White to criticize sociologists for alleged anthropomorphism, and psychologists for not realizing that psychological processes cannot explain cultural traits, and the like. For on White's theory that the culture, not the individual, is always responsible, sociologists are not guilty of anthropomorphism, the culture is guilty. Robert Lynd really did not say that culture does not "enamel its fingernails, or vote, or believe in capitalism, but people do"; the *culture* enunciated that doctrine. Nor did V. Gordon Childe really say that "changes in culture . . . can be   initiated, controlled, or delayed by the conscious and deliberate choice of their human authors and executors." No, on White's doctrine, the culture said it.

No matter what evidence or counter-examples one cites in reply to White's doctrine that the culture, not the individual, is responsible for any changes in culture or human behavior, White will not allow them to count as evidence against his thesis; he arbitrarily protects the thesis against refutation. This is a dogmatic way to hold a claim, and it indicates that here again White defends a view *not* as if it were an hypothesis to which empirical evidence is relevant, but rather in such a way as to transform it into a purely verbal device.

The thesis which White is really insisting upon (though it gets confused with some other claims) is that we should (try to) understand cultural phenomena in terms of their origins. He insists that to explain any social or cultural phenomena, we must find the cultural antecedents (and concomitants, he sometimes adds). At times White writes as though once the cultural antecedents are known, the phenomena is understood; there is nothing more to seek. Instead of regarding knowledge of cultural antecedents simply as a *necessary* condition, he treats it as *sufficient* for understanding. But this is a mistake. For the consequences of cultural practices are important for understanding also. Simply seeing the cultural antecedents of a practice may not give us this information. A traditional practice may take on new functions, fulfill new and different purposes. Though the analogy is not exact, it is useful to point out that those who are best acquainted with the antecedents of contemporary physics, anthropology, or sociology (historians of these subjects) may not necessarily have the best understanding of current developments in these fields.

One particularly unhappy example of White's attempt to treat subjects in terms of origins is his theory of human beliefs. White (1949: 349fn.) writes:

> Philosophies possess, hold, animate, guide and direct the articulate, protoplasmic mechanisms that are men. Whether a man—an average man, typical of his group—"believes in" Christ or Buddha, Genesis or Geology, Determinism or Free Will, is not a matter of his own choosing. His philosophy is merely the response of his neuro-sensory-muscular-glandular system to the streams of cultural stimuli impinging upon him from the outside. What is called "philosophizing" is merely the interaction of these cultural elements within his organism. His "choice" of philosophic beliefs is merely a neurological expression of the superior strength of some of these extrasomatic cultural forces.

So, a reader of White's articles and books does not have a choice of whether to become a cultural determinist or not. Are we to wait until we are "possessed" by culturology, or should we do some things which will put us in a better position to get "possessed?" But if we did the latter, *we* wouldn't have done it; since we couldn't possibly have chosen to do so, the culture did it to us.

In order to further his claim that culture controls man, White cites paragraphs from the writings of Darwin and Poincaré in which these men wrote about cases in which it did *not* seem to them that *they* provided the vital ideas. But what White ignores is the fact that they could report such events only because they could contrast these cases with others in which they *did* figure out the important theories. So that White's emphasis, designed to further his theory that the culture is always responsible, never the individual, is a half truth which needs to be corrected in the light of a wider body of evidence.

We generally assume that whether or not an hypothesis is correct, or more probable than its alternatives, is a matter to be decided by reflection upon the available evidence. In the latter process one sees, among other things, the logical implications of the proposition (s) in question, the way in which each relates to others we already know, and the like. Now one reason why we believe deliberation does occur in some cases is that by contrast there are other instances in which views are accepted quite arbitrarily. Some voting in university faculty meetings occurs after careful committee work and deliberation. But in some other cases the voting approaches the ideal limit of the perfectly arbitrary or thoughtless, because no one cares much what the outcome may be; the issues are not deemed important.

Given White's own theory, it would follow that White's "choice" of cultural determinism (and his other beliefs) is "merely a neurological expression of the superior strength of . . . cultural forces." Does his view of beliefs as merely due to the strength of certain cultural forces imply that it makes no sense to talk about the *truth* of human beliefs and whether there is adequate evidence for them? If so, this is intellectual nihilism, and White's theory of beliefs has consequences as dangerous for White's theories (beliefs) as for those of anyone else.

It is necessary to distinguish between the cause (or causes) of a belief, and the grounds for the belief (those reasons which could honestly be offered in its support). There are cases in which the major causal factor in the acceptance of a belief was the fact that a person had that belief instilled in him in his home environment; there may be or may not be evidence in support of that belief; the truth of, or warrant for, the belief is a separate question from the environmental influences which led him to hold the view. The confusion of the origins or cause of a belief with the truth of a belief is known as the genetic fallacy.

When White sees that his doctrines that culture controls man and that man can only react to culture are not wholly persuasive, he employs two strategies. First, in two uncharacteristic, isolated passages he denies that his thesis *means* what it clearly seems to mean. White (1949:174) writes that his view of the relation of culture and man does *not* require that the individual organism be viewed as a passive thing.

> The individual does not receive cultural material from the outside in a purely passive way, like a cup into which coffee is poured, not does it reflect this material like a perfect mirror does an image. The human organism is a *dynamic* system. It not only receives cultural elements from the outside, it *acts* upon them . . . We do not . . . minimize the dynamic nature of the individual as an active as well as a reactive organism. We are merely saying that a consideration of the dynamic character of this organism does not help us to explain the form and content of its reactions and responses.

This disclaimer cannot be taken seriously as a representative statement of White's position because White's endlessly repeated claim that "man cannot control culture but culture controls man" has the effect of insisting that man *does merely* receive cultural elements from outside, he does *not* act upon them. In the second odd passage, White (1949:176fn.) writes that "Any response of the human organism is the result of countless antecedent and concomitant events that we may term 'causes.' The human organism is constantly organizing and synthesizing these causative factors on the one hand, and expressing the resultant behavior overtly on the other." But if the claim that "culture controls man, and man cannot control culture" means anything at all, its author cannot consistently admit that the human organism can organize and synthesize causal factors. It is no wonder that White does not account for this human activity. If he should say that this task belongs to psychology, not culturology, the reply is that even the psychologist could not predict or explain such behavior if he had to assume doctrines which in effect deny that it can occur.

White's second strategy (1949:173), when pressed, is to shift from the claim that culture controls man to the weaker thesis that *whatever* men do—whether they absorb their culture *or* alter it, they do so because their culture has provided the elements which make possible their activities; their actions are outgrowths of cultural traits. Now it should be pointed out that to say that all human behavior (of interest to the science of culture) is due to overt, external cultural traits can neither be proved nor disproved. Instead of regarding it as a factual proposition which is true or false, it should be converted into an imperative which functions as a heuristic device: always try to find the cultural antecedents of the behavior; if you don't at first succeed, keep trying and you probably will.

What White should have said, but did not, is that the approach which regards individuals' achievements as a product of cultural patterns of considerable scope and depth is *one* legitimate approach, and that it lends itself to striking predictions and explanations of human behavior not otherwise obtainable. Had White shown that on the basis of this approach he and others had made non-vague predictions, which were later fulfilled, and explained cultural phenomena in such a way as to withstand critical examination, then he would have been in a good position to say that his approach is warranted. But he has fulfilled neither of these conditions,[5] yet he continues to theorize as though his culturology were all-sufficient.

Summary

In examining White's assertion that culture controls man, we found that the claim should have been set forth as an hypothesis, and then modified in the light of a comprehensive examination of the evidence. Instead it was presented and held dogmatically. The effect of such a procedure is to frustrate instead of to fulfill the expectation that the requirements for a *science* will be met.

When we inspect the evidence which White supplies for the theory that man cannot control culture, we see that the proposition can only mean that humans, either as individuals or as groups, cannot deliberately change culture traits, such as tools or techniques. But we saw that in fact men have made such significant planned changes, so that White's thesis does not withstand examination.

On White's view, no matter whether the group ossifies certain culture traits or introduces new techniques or tools to replace the old, it is simply *reacting* to its culture. This view reminds us of that type of theological position which says no matter whether the sparrow flies or dies, God caused it. Both positions are equally *ad hoc;* both are stated in such a way that no possible evidence could count against them and thus they are guaranteed against refutation. But this very fact shows that neither of them is a scientific hypothesis.

This paper does not consider some very significant views with which White has been prominently identified, e.g., evolutionary and energy theories. The topics discussed herein, however, are illustrative of the kinds of problems which must be surmounted if White's theories are to meet the requirements for a genuine science.

NOTES

[1]Time for study and writing of the present paper was made possible by a Charles Merrill Foundation grant. I am indebted to Professors George P. Murdock, Arthur Tuden, Frank Young, and Louise Sweet for reading and discussing with me the earlier version of this paper.

[2]In this context "first type" means simply first in the list of evidences given by White in his frequently reprinted essay, "Man's Control Over Civilization: An Anthropocentric Illusion."

[3]This sounds much like the voice of the paradigm of social and political conservatism, Edmund Burke, speaking again but in the twentieth century, this time in the clothes of an anthropologist. It is *as if* White were using anthropology to further (preordained?) political doctrines.

[4]White distinguishes between culture and behavior most sharply or forcefully in his 1959 essay, "The Concept of Culture."

[5]See Steward (1960) concerning White's explanations.

In the version of history that most of us learned as school-children, important discoveries and inventions were the creations of particular "geniuses," without whose unique talents civilization would never have progressed to its present state. Ignored or passed over lightly was the fact that virtually every major discovery or invention in history was arrived at independently by two or more individuals within a short time of one another. Indeed, this has occurred with such regularity that Obgurn and Thomas ask, "Are inventions inevitable?" Their discussion of this question is followed by an impressive list of 148 duplicate independent inventions. As they point out, the list could easily be extended through further historical research. A recent instance of this phenomenon is the independent invention of the artificial heart by entertainer Paul Winchell and medical researcher Dr. Willem Kolff.

For further discussion of the problem of invention, we recommend Leslie A. White's "Genius: Its Causes and Incidence" (1949: 190-232) and Robert Merton's "Singleton and Multiples in Scientific Discovery: A Chapter in the Sociology of Science" (1961). Kroeber's (1919; B-M, A-137) and Kroeber and Richardson's (1940; most easily available in Hammel and Simmons' 1970: 126-137) work on changes in women's fashions is also of interest here.

One: 5

Are Inventions Inevitable?
A Note on Social Evolution

*William F. Ogburn and Dorothy Thomas**

It is an interesting phenomenon that many inventions have been made two or more times by different inventors, each working without knowledge of the other's research. There are a number of cases of such duplicate inventions or discoveries that are of common knowledge. It is well known, for instance, that both Newton and Leibnitz invented calculus. The theory of natural selection was developed practically identically by Wallace and by Darwin. It is claimed that both Langley and Wright invented the airplane. And we all know that the telephone was invented by Gray and by Bell. A good many such cases of duplication in discovery are part of the stock of knowledge of the general reader.

There are, however, a large number of very important instances that are not so well known. For example, the invention of decimal fractions is credited to Rudolph, Stevinus and Bürgi. Oxygen was discovered by Scheele and by Priestley in 1774. The molecular theory is due to Avagadro in 1811 and to Ampère in 1814. Both Cros and du Hauron invented color photography in 1869. The trolley car resulted from the work of Van Doeple and also Sprague, and the essential elements were devised independently by Siemens and Daft.

We think of Napier and Briggs as the inventors of logarithms, but it is not generally known that Bürgi also invented them three years previously. We associate the origin of photography with Daguerre but it was also independently invented by Talbot. Boyle's law is known in French textbooks as Marriotte's Law. The existence of Neptune was discovered independently by Adams and Leverrier, before the planet was actually observed, the work of these two mathe-

---

*Reprinted with permission from the *Political Science Quarterly*, 37 (March 1922), pp. 83-98.

The late William F. Ogburn and Dorothy Thomas were sociologists at Columbia University.

matical astronomers leading to its observation by others. Gauss is frequently recognized as responsible for the principle of least squares. Legendre published his account of the principle three years before Gauss did, although Gauss had used the principle still earlier.

There were four independent discoveries of sunspots, all in 1611, namely, by Galileo in Italy, Scheiner in Germany, Fabricius in Holland and Harriott in England. The law of the conservation of energy, so significant in science and philosophy, was formulated four times independently in 1847, by Joule, Thomson, Colding and Helmholz. They had been anticipated by Robert Mayer in 1842. There seem to have been at least six different inventors of the thermometer and no less than nine claimants of the invention of the telescope. Type writing machines were invented simultaneously in England and in America by several individuals in these countries. The steamboat is claimed as the "exclusive" discovery of Fulton, Jouffroy, Rumsey, Stevens and Symmington.

That so many inventions and discoveries were made by two or more persons is not generally known. Researches into the histories of science and of inventions reveal a surprisingly large number of instances of multiple but independent origins of inventions. The appendix to this article contains a list of 148 such cases chosen from the fields of mathematics, astronomy, chemistry, physics, medicine, biology, psychology and practical mechanics. The list could be extended considerably by further research, particularly into the fields of lesser inventions. The best source for such data is the history of science within the past hundred years. The origin of the vast number of minor inventions in the practical arts is not recorded except within recent years in the files of the patent offices.

Knowledge of the origins of inventions in early times is lost. Records are largely dependent on writing, and it is only in recent years that we have written information about inventors. Among the peoples without writing there were probably many independent inventions of the same tool. But definite proof is difficult to obtain because it is not easy to tell whether the possession of the same tool by two different primitive groups is due to diffusion or to independent origin. In some cases the probability of independent origin is very great, as in the case of bronze-making in Peru and in the Old World, or the blowgun in America and in Borneo, or the pyramids in Central America and in Egypt. A fairly long list of such instances might be cited. But a statistical compilation of probable instances of multiple origins of inventions among primitive peoples would give little evidence of the relative frequency of inventions made independently, because of the vast number of cases about which we are ignorant.

But, if we leave these cases out of consideration and confine our evidence merely to the historical period, it is surprising that we can find so many cases where two or more inventors independently made the same invention, for the development of contacts has made the spread of knowledge increasingly rapid. For instance, if the knowledge of the invention of wireless telegraphy is spread quickly over all the industrialized areas, this fact in itself would cut short the researches of other inventors along similar lines. Furthermore, many inventions and discoveries are now patented, so that the invention of the same object by others either is prevented, or, if not prevented, is known. The records of the United States Patent Office show that about twice as many patents are applied for as are granted. Many of these applications are no doubt denied because the invention is already patented. This is further evidence that many inventions are made independently by more than one person.

For all these reasons a list of recurring independent inventions assumes a greater importance than would be apparent otherwise, and a list of inventions made only once would not only be of little significance but would not imply that, without the patent laws and rapid dissemination of knowledge, they would necessarily have been invented only once. In trying to form some estimate, therefore, of the frequency of inventions occurring independently more than once, one should remember these limitations on the interpretation of the data.

Bearing in mind all these considerations, the list given in the appendix to this article is very impressive. What does it mean? Several questions are raised. Are inventions inevitable? If the various inventors had died in infancy, would not the inventions have been made and would not cultural progress have gone on without much delay? Are inventions independent of mental ability? Is not the determinism in inventions a matter of cultural preparation? Is not social evolution inherent in the nature of culture?

The significance of the phenomenon of parallel occurrences of the same inventions has been been ably discussed by Dr. A. L. Kroeber (1917) and the answers to such questions as the foregoing have been considered by him. In general, the theory turns on two points; that is, there are two factors in the making of inventions, mental ability and the existing status of culture.

Mental ability, it is thought, is related to invention in somewhat the following manner. There is little doubt that inventors are men of con-

siderable mental ability, except, perhaps, in instances where the accidental element is large. The measurement of the mental ability of the individuals in any large sample of the general population shows a distribution resembling the familiar normal probability curve. For any
particular mental trait there are only a few with large measurements
and only a few with small measurements and a great many individuals
in between. The distribution of mental traits is similar, for example,
to the distribution of statures, in which there are few who are tall and
few who are short and many with medium stature, the distribution
being continuous. Inventors no doubt come from the upper portion of
such a frequency distribution of ability.

Of course, we do not know just how high up in the scale of ability
the inventor is found. But in a large sample the normal probability
curve is such that, in the upper half of the scale of ability, will be
found half the number of cases. The distribution above the upper
third of the scale will usually include about one-quarter of the cases.
That is to say, out of 1000 individuals about 225 on the average will
be found above the upper third of the scale; and about 10 will be
found above the upper tenth of the scale. Thus, even granting that the
mental ability of the inventor is great, the probabilities are that out of
a large sample there are many chances of finding more than one person with a high degree of native ability. So that, if an inventor had
died as an infant, there are chances that there are others with just as
high native inventive ability.

But ability may vary over a period of time as well as in a cross-section
of time. Thus, a random sample of 1000 individuals taken 500 years
ago may have measured in inherited mental traits higher or lower in the
scale than 1000 individuals chosen today. The average may be greater
or less. We are here considering native or inherited ability, not the
ability that results from training. Any high-school boy today knows
more mathematics than did Aristotle, but his native ability in mathematics is probably much less. The way this native ability will vary
over time will be by mutations or by selection. Mutations are very in-
frequent and the process of selection is also slow;[1] so that reckoning
four generations to the century and considering the fact that a biological change or mutation must spread to a large number of individuals,
there cannot be very much variation by groups in inherited mental
ability over a few centuries. Therefore over the few centuries of historical period, or at least over the period for which we can get data on
the origin of inventions, the variation in native ability according to
time may in all probability be neglected. There is of course—to repeat

—variation within a definite sample, but the nature of the distribution of native ability is such that there is considerable probability of finding more than one individual with the particular native inventive ability. In fact such native ability may be quite plentiful.

On the other hand, the second factor in invention, the status of culture, is obviously highly variable over time, particularly in the last few centuries. The material culture three hundred years ago was very different from what it is now. It has changed rapidly. And the elements of the material culture at any one time have a good deal to do with determining the nature of the particular inventions that are made. For instance, a few discoveries regarding electricity made possible a great many inventions in which these fundamental discoveries were used or applied. The many electrical appliances could not have been invented in, let us say, the fifteenth century, because the fundamental discoveries regarding electricity had not been made. A certain cultural preparation was quite necessary for the invention of the telegraph. The fact that so many electrical inventions followed so quickly after certain researches in electricity had been made, suggests the inevitability of these inventions. And also the fact that most of the major electrical inventions were made by two or more inventors leads one to think that electrical development was more dependent on cultural preparation than on genius. Benjamin (1901:iii) says in the introduction to his *Age of Electricity:* "It is a singular fact that probably not an electrical invention of major importance has ever been made but that the honor of its origin has been claimed by more than one person." In 1745, Dean von Kleist found that by inserting an electrified wire into a phial containing spirits of wine, he could store electricity. The same experiment was made the following year by Cuneus of Leyden, and thus we have the fundamental principle of the Leyden jar. The French claim that D'Alibard was the first to discover the identity of lightning and electricity. He performed in May, 1752, the same experiment that Benjamin Franklin performed in June of the same year. The electrical effects of dissimilar metals had been noted by Sulzer in 1768 and Cotuguo in 1786, but the effective discovery was not made until 1791 when Galvani independently discovered these same results and evolved the principle of the voltaic or galvanic cell, first constructed by Volta.

The successful invention of the telegraph was the culmination of many abortive attempts to transmit electricity. The first record of any practical form of electric telegraph is described in *The Scots Magazine* in 1783 in an article supposedly written by Charles Marshal. In 1787,

Lomond proposed a similar but more practical plan. The invention of the galvanometer by Ampère and the electro-magnet by Arago then gave a tremendous impetus and in 1831 a young American professor, Joseph Henry, constructed the first electro-magnetic telegraph. Henry did not patent his idea or make it public, and important as the invention was, it remained hidden until Morse performed his experiments in 1837 and finally put his telegraph in operation in 1844. It may be questioned whether Morse is entitled to the credit for the invention, since he neither first devised the mechanism nor originated the alphabet. There were two other inventors. Cook and Wheatstone obtained a patent in England in 1837, as a result of their joint experiments in constructing a telegraph; and just a month afterward, as a result of independent investigations, Steinheil successfully constructed a telegraph in Munich. Thus the evolution of electrical science was in the direction of the telegraph, and the invention was not dependent upon any one inventor.

Electric motors appeared simultaneously in England, France, Germany, Italy and the United States; and dal Negro, Joseph Henry, Bourbonze, McGawley and Davenport all laid claim to the invention. Given the railroad and electric motors, is not the electric railroad inevitable? At least six different men, Davidson, Jacobi, Lilly, Davenport, Page and Hall, claim to have made independently the application of electricity to the railroad. Similar inquiries show that the development of science was leading up to the following inventions, each one of which was invented by several different inventors: the induction coil, the secondary battery, the electrolysis of water, the electro-deposition of metals, the ring armature, the microphone, the self-exciting dynamo, the incandescent light and the telephone. Such a record of electrical inventions, while not negativing the factor of mental ability, certainly shows quite impressively the importance of the cultural factors.

We realize, of course, that the invention of the steamboat was dependent upon the invention of the boat and the invention of the steam engine. The dependence of an invention upon its constituent elements is a fact. The constituent elements are each in turn dependent on their constituent elements, and so on back to the ice ages and to resources of nature. But does the existence of all the constituent elements of an invention make that invention inevitable? Given the boat and the steam engine, is not the steamboat inevitable?

This tendency toward the inevitability of an invention, once given the constituent parts, and the dependence of the invention on these parts, may be seen in the history of the steam engine (Thurston 1902). One sees in the interesting development of the steam engine that this invention was not dependent upon any one man and the history indicates that no one man could be expected to invent the various constituent parts as preliminary steps to making the culminating invention.

Omitting from consideration the earlier origins of the steam engine, we may start with Rivault, who proved in 1605 by experiment that water confined in a bomb-shell and heated would explode the shell. Porta had previously described an aparatus by which the pressure of steam could be made to raise a column of water. In 1615 de Caus constructed a machine similar to the one described by Porta. In 1630 Ramseye patented a "steam machine." This period was devoted largely to speculations as to the possibilities of steam and no further practical application was attempted until 1663, when Worcester constructed a machine similar to those of Porta and of de Caus, and used it to elevate water at Vauxhall. Hautefeuille in 1678 proposed the use of a piston in the steam engine and Huygens first applied this principle. Engines which were a decided improvement on Worcester's were now built. Great interest was aroused in their possibilities, and many minds set to work to solve the "problem of the steam engine." An important advance was made by Thomas Savery, who in 1698 patented a design for the first engine used in pumping water from mines. Improvements on Savery's engine were made by Desaguliers in 1718, by Blakely and Ridgeley in 1756, 'and also by Papin about this time. Thurston remarks that "at the beginning of the eighteenth century, every element of the modern steam engine had been separately invented and practically applied" (*op. cit.*:55). The nature of the vacuum and the method of obtaining it were known. Steam boilers capable of sustaining any desired pressure had been made. The piston had been utilized and the safety valve invented. Thomas Newcomen constructed a new type of engine combining these elements instead of attempting an improvement on Savery's. His invention was "the engine of Huygens with its cylinder and piston as improved by Papin, still further improved by Newcomen and Calley by the addition of the method of condensation used in the Savery engine" (*op. cit.*:60). From Newcomen to Watt there were improvements in proportions and alterations of details. Watt experimented with the Newcomen engine, discovered sources of loss of heat, and set about to eliminate this waste. The Watt engine was given its distinctive form by 1785, and since that time the growth of the steam engine has not been great, the changes being in the nature of minor improvements. Contrary to popular impression, Watt, great man though he was, does not seem to have been indispensable to the perfection of the steam engine. It would be an absurdity to conclude that, even if he had died in infancy, the Industrial Revolution would not have occurred.

Our analysis and the list of multiple inventions indicates the great importance of the status of culture as a factor in the origin of inventions. While it is true that inventions are in large part culturally determined, this fact does not mean that we can at the present stage of our information predict a particular time. In some cases the probability of predicting an invention is strong as, for instance, in the case of the steamboat, which was invented by Fulton eighteen years after the perfection of the steam engine in 1785. But in most cases we do not know fully enough the cultural situation determining the invention. To say that culture is a determining factor in inventions does not tell us what are the particular elements and conditions.[2] We do not always know beforehand what the necessary constituent cultural elements are that go into the making of an invention.

But even if these elements are in existence and if there is also the necessary native ability, the mental ability and the constituent cultural elements must be brought together. Inherent ability may exist but it must receive the necessary cultural training and it must be applied. The problem has to be seen, its solution socially desired and the ability must be trained and stimulated to attack the problem. This is where the idea of necessity, so commonly associated with the conception of inventiveness, comes in. Necessity will not produce an invention without the existence of the essential elements. For example, there was most urgent necessity among our forefathers not many generations ago to cure illness and prevent death. They tried magic and the use of herbs; but the science of medicine had not been developed; the cultural preparation did not exist. The need of an invention has a great deal to do with bringing ability and the cultural elements together, and is an important factor in the process, but there must exist the cultural preparation.

In conclusion, it is thought that the evidence presented of independent duplicate origins of inventions brings out forcibly the importance of the cultural factor in the production of inventions. Such data challenge us to analyze the relation of mental ability and cultural preparation as factors in the origin of inventions. To say that one of these factors is more important than the other is to condense the conclusion to unwarranted brevity. It is more satisfactory to summarize briefly the way these two factors are related. Mental ability is a factor, since no inventions could be made without it. And the mental ability of inventors is above the average. But the distribution of inherent mental ability at any one time is such that there is great probability of considerable frequency of exceptional native ability. The manifest ability necessary to produce inventions may be rare because the native ability has not been trained or applied to the problems of inventions. On the other hand, a specific invention depends upon a certain cultural preparation, and could not be made without the existence of the constituent cultural elements that make the invention.

However, if the necessary constituent elements exist, the invention may occur if there is a cultural need for it, for at any one time the distribution of inherent mental ability is such that in a large sample there are many cases of exceptional native mental ability. Witness the frequency of multiple independent inventions. Furthermore, the variation in a result, e.g., in inventions, depends on the variation of the factors. The factor of culture, since the historical period, varies rapidly within very short periods of time. The constituent elements of culture at any one time are different from what they were a few years previously. No such variation is conceivable in inherent mental ability over so short a time. In fact, it is exceedingly probable that over a few centuries there is no appreciable variation in the average or the distribution of inherited mental ability. The evidence and analysis show the tremendous importance of the cultural factor for inventions. Since the existing status of culture is so important a determinant of a succeeding culture, since culture is so highly variable, since inherited mental ability is so stable, we must conclude that the processes of cultural evolution are to be explained in cultural and social terms, that is, in terms of sociology and not in terms of biology and psychology.

Appendix
A List of Some Inventions and Discoveries Made Independently by Two or More Persons

The accompanying list of duplicate independent inventions is collected from histories of astronomy, mathematics, chemistry, physics, electricity, physiology, biology, psychology and practical mechanical inventions. The data are thus from the period of written records, indeed the last few centuries, and largely from histories of science. The various inventions and discoveries vary greatly in their importance. The list could be extended by further research.

There are disputes concerning many of the origins in the instances listed. Disputes frequently concern priority, a matter with which the accompanying discussion is not concerned. Where a date is doubtful a question-mark has been placed after it. Occasionally we have not been able to get the date. The most serious difficulty in making the list is the fact that the contribution of one person is in some cases more complete than that of another. For instance, Laplace's account of the nebular hypothesis is in more scientific detail than Kant's. Similarly, Halley's role may not have been as important as Newton's in formulating the law of inverse squares. It is sometimes doubtful just where to draw the lines defining a new contribution. Our guides have been the histories of science, and where there are differences in the historical accounts we have followed the general practice. The case of the discovery of the circulation of the blood we have excluded, as there seems to be a rather wide difference in the contributions of Cesalpino (1571) and Harvey (1776). Although our rule has been to exclude such cases of doubt, in some instances where they have been included we have placed a question mark next to the name. In several cases the independence of the research of one claimant has been questioned by another claimant or by his followers. In many cases the verdict on the controversy seems to be that each of the inventors justly deserves the distinction. Such is the case with the Newton-Leibnitz controversy over calculus, and the Torricelli-Roberval controversy on the cycloid. In the case of the microscope, telescope, thermometer, steamboat, electric railways and others, claims are still matters of dispute. In a few cases we have indicated this fact by the words "claimed by" following the subject of the discovery or invention. Most of the cases of widely different dates have special explanations as in the case of Mendel, and numerous cases where the first inventor does not publish his theory until other have come to some conclusions, e.g., there is indisputable evidence that Young discovered the principle of interference thirteen years before Fresnel, yet neglected to publish it. It has also been difficult to abbreviate the description of the discovery into a short title suitable for a list.

I

1. Solution of the problem of three bodies. By Clairaut (1747), Euler (1747) and D'Alembert (1747).
2. Theory of the figure of the earth. By Huygens (1690) and Newton (1680?).
3. Variability of satellites. By Bradley (1752) and Wargentin (1746).
4. Motion of light within the earth's orbit. By Delambre (1821?) and Bradley (1728).

5. Theory of planetary perturbations. By Lagrange (1808) and Laplace (1808).
6. Discovery of the planet Neptune. By Adams (1845) and Leverrier (1845).
7. Discovery of sun spots. By Galileo (1611), Fabricius (1611), Scheiner (1611) and Harriott (1611).
8. Law of inverse squares. By Newton (1666) and Halley (1684).
9. Nebular hypothesis. By Laplace (1796) and Kant (1755).
10. Effect of tidal friction on motion of the earth. By Ferrel (1853) and Delaunay (1853).
11. Correlation between variations of sun spots and disturbances on the earth. By Sabine (1852), Wolfe (1852) and Gauthier (1852).
12. Method of getting spectrum at edge of sun's disc. By Jannsen (1868) and Lockyer (1868).
13. Discovery of the inner ring of Saturn. By Bond (1850) and Dawes (1850).
14. First measurement of the parallax of a star. By Bessell (1838), Struve (1838) and Henderson (1838).
15. The effect of gravitation on movements of the ocean. By Lenz (1845?) and Carpenter (1865).
16. Certain motions of the moon. By Clairaut (1752), Euler (1752) and D'Alembert (1752).

II

17. Decimal fractions. By Stevinus (1585), Bürgi (1592), Beyer? (1603) and Rüdolff? (1530).
18. Introduction of decimal point. By Bürgi (1592), Pitiscus (1608-12), Kepler (1616) and Napier (1616-17).
19. The equation of the cycloid. By Torricelli (1644) and Roberval (1640).
20. Logarithms. By Bürgi (1620) and Napier-Briggs (1614).
21. The tangent of the cycloid. By Viviani (1660?), Descartes (1660?) and Fermat (1660?).
22. Calculus. By Newton (1671) and Leibnitz (1676).
23. The rectification of the semi-cubical parabola. By Van Heuraet (1659), Neil (1657) and Fermat (1657-9).
24. Deduction of the theorem on the hexagon. By Pascal (1639), MacLaurin (1719-20) and Bessel (1820).
25. The principle of least squares. By Gauss (1809) and Legendre (1806).

26. The geometric law of duality. By Poncelet (1838) and Gergone (1838).
27. The beginnings of synthetic projective geometry. By Chasles (1830) and Steiner (1830).
28. Geometry with an axiom contradictory to Euclid's parallel axiom. By Lobatchevsky (1836-40?), Boylais (1826-33) and Gauss? (1829).
29. Lobatchevsky's doctrine of the parallel angle. By Lobatchevsky (1840) and Saccheri (1733).
30. Method of algebraic elimination by use of determinants and by dialitic method. By Hesse (1842) and Sylvester (1840).
31. A treatment of vectors without the use of coordinate systems. By Hamilton (1843), Grassman (1843) and others (1843).
32. Principle of uniform convergence. By Stokes (1847-8) and Seidel (1847-8).
33. Logarithmic criteria for convergence of series. By Abel, De Morgan, Bertrand, Raabe, Duhamel, Bonnet, Paucker (all between 1832-51).
34. Radix method of making logarithms. By Briggs (1624), Flower (1771), Atwood (1786), Leonelli (1802) and Manning (1806).
35. Circular slide rule. By Delamain (1630) and Oughtred (1632).
36. Method of indivisibles. By Roberval (1640?) and Cavalieri (1635).
37. Researches on elliptic functions. By Abel (1826-29), Jacobi (1829) and Legendre (1811-28).
38. The double theta functions. By Gopel (1847) and Rosenhain (1847).
39. The law of quadratic reciprocity. By Gauss (1788-96), Euler (1737) and Legendre (1830).
40. The application of the potential function to mathematical theory of electricity and magnetism. By Green (1828), Thomson (1846), Chasles, Sturm and Gauss.
41. Dirichlet's principle in the theory of potentials. By Dirichlet (1848?) and Thomson (1848).
42. Contraction hypothesis. By H. A. Lorentz (1895) and Fitzgerald (1895).
43. Mathematical calculation of the size of molecules. By Loschmidt and Thompson.

III

44. Structure theory. By Butlerow (1888), Kekule (1888) and Couper (1888).

45. Law of gases. By Boyle (1662) and Marriotte (1676).
46. Discovery of oxygen. By Scheele (1774) and Priestley (1774).
47. Liquification of oxygen. By Cailletet (1877) and Pictet (1877).
48. Method of liquefying gases. By Cailletet, Pictet, Wroblowski and Olzewski (all between 1877-1884).
49. Estimation of proportion of oxygen in atmosphere. By Scheele (1778) and Cavendish (1781).
50. Beginnings of modern organic chemistry. By Boerhave (1732) and Hales (1732).
51. Isolation of nitrogen. By Rutherford (1772) and Scheele (1773).
52. That water is produced by combustion of hydrogen. By Lavoisier-Laplace (1783) and Cavendish (1784).
53. Law of chemical proportions. By Proust (1801-9) and Richter (?).
54. The periodic law: First arrangement of atoms in ascending series. By DeChancourtois (1864), Newlands (1864) and Lothar Meyer (1864). Law of periodicity. By Lothar Meyer (1869) and Mendeleeff (1869).
55. Hypothesis as to arrangement of atoms in space. By Van't Hoff (1874) and Le Bel (1874).
56. Molecular theory. By Ampère (1814) and Avagadro (1811).
57. Hydrogen acid theory. By Davy and Du Long.
58. Doctrine of chemical equivalents. By Wenzel (1777) and Richter (1792).
59. Discovery of element of phosphorus. By Brand (1669), Kunckel (1678) and Boyle (1680).
60. Discovery of boron. By Davy (1808-9) and Gay-Lussac (1808).
61. Discovery of ceria. By Hisinger (1803), Berzelius (1803-4) and Klaproth (1803-4).
62. Process for reduction of aluminum. By Hall (1886), Heroult (1887) and Cowles (1885).
63. Law of mass action of chemical forces. By Jellet (1873), Guldberg-Waage (1867), Van't Hoff (1877) and others.
64. Comparison of refractivity of equimolecular quantities by multiple function. By L. V. Lorenz (1880) and H. A. Lorentz (1880).

IV

65. Resistance of vacuum. By Torricelli-Pascal (1643-6) and von Gutericke (1657).
66. Air gun. By Boyle-Hooke (prior to 1659) and von Guericke (1650).
67. Telescope. Claimed by Lippershey (1608), Della Porta (1558), Digges (1571), Johannides, Metius (1608), Drebbel, Fontana, Jansen (1608) and Galileo (1609).

68. Microscope. Claimed by Johannides, Drebbel and Galileo (1610?).
69. Acromatic lens. By Hall (1729) and Dolland (1758).
70. Principle of interference. By Young (1802) and Fresnel (1815).
71. Spectrum analysis. By Draper (1860), Angstrom (1854), Kirchoff-Bunsen (1859), Miller (1843) and Stokes (1849).
72. Photography. By Daguerre-Niepe (1839) and Talbot (1839).
73. Color photography. By Cros (1869) and Du Hauron (1869).
74. Discovery of overtones in strings. By Nobb-Pigott (1677) and Sauveur (1700-03).
75. Thermometer. Claimed by Galileo (1592-7?), Drebbel? (1608), Sanctorious (1612), Paul (1617), Fludd (1617), Van Guericke, Porta (1606), De Caus (1615).
76. Pendulum clock. Claimed by Bürgi (1575), Galileo (1582) and Huygens (1656).
77. Discovery of latent heat. By Black (1762), De Luc and Wilke.
78. Ice calorimeter. By Lavoisier, Laplace (1780) and Black-Wilke.
79. Law of expansion of gases. By Charles (1783) and Gay-Lussac (1802).
80. Continuity of gaseous and liquid states of matter. By Ramsay (1880) and Jamin (1883).
81. Kinetic theory of gases. By Clausius (1850) and Rankine (1850).
82. Law of conservation of energy. By Mayer (1843), Joule (1847), Helmholz (1847), Colding (1847) and Thomson (1847).
83. Mechanical equivalent of heat. By Mayer (1842), Carnot (1830), Seguin (1839) and Joule (1840).
84. Principle of dissipation of energy. By Carnot? (1824), Clausius (1850) and Thomson (1852).
85. Law of impact, earlier conclusions. By Galileo (1638) and Marci (1639).
86. Laws of mutual impact of bodies. By Huygens (1669), Wallis (1668) and Wren (1668).
87. Apparent concentration of cold by concave mirror. By Porta (1780-91?) and Pictet (1780-91?).
88. Circumstances by which effect of weight is determined. By Leonardo and Ubaldi.
89. Parallelogram of forces. By Newton (1687) and Varignon (1725?).
90. Principle of hydrostatics. By Archimedes and Stevinus (1608).
91. Pneumatic lever. By Hamilton (1835) and Barker (1832).
92. Osmotic pressure methods. By Van't Hoff (1886) and Guldberg (1870).

93. Law of inertia. By Galileo, Huygens and Newton (1687).
94. Machinery for verifying the law of falling bodies. By Laborde, Lippich and von Babo.
95. Center of oscillation. By Bernouilli (1712) and Taylor (1715).

V

96. Leyden jar. By von Kleist (1745) and Cuneus (1746).
97. Discovery of animal electricity. By Sultzer (1768), Cotuguo (1786) and Galvani (1791).
98. Telegraph. By Henry (1831), Morse (1837), Cooke-Wheatstone (1837) and Steinheil (1837).
99. Electric motors. Claimed by Dal Negro (1830), Henry (1831), Bourbonze and McGawley (1835).
100. Electric railroad. Claimed by Davidson, Jacobi, Lilly-Colton (1847), Davenport (1835), Page (1850) and Hall (1850-1).
101. Induction coil. By Page and Ruhmkorff.
102. Secondary battery. By Ritter and Planté (1859).
103. Electrolysis of water. By Nicholson-Carlisle (1800) and Ritter.
104. Method of converting lines engraved on copper into relief. By Jacobi (1839), Spencer (1839) and Jordan (1839).
105. Ring armature. By Pacinotti (1864) and Gramme (1860).
106. Microphone. Hughes (1878), Edison (1877-8), Berliner (1877) and Blake? (1878).
107. The phonograph. By Edison (1877), Scott? and Cross (1877).
108. Self-exciting dynamo. Claimed by Hjorth (1866-7), Varley (1866-7), Siemens (1866-7), Wheatstone (1866-7), Ladd (1866) and Wilde (1863-7).
109. Incandescent electric light. Claimed by Starr (1846) and Jobard de Clangey (1838).
110. Telephone. By Bell (1876) and Gray (1876).
111. Arrest of electro-magnetic waves. By Branley (1890-1), Lodge (1893) and Hughes (1880).
112. Electro-magnetic clocks. By Wheatstone (1845) and Bain (1845).
113. Printing telegraphs. By Wheatstone (1845) and Bain (1845).

VI

114. Theory of the infection of micro-organisms. By Fracastoro (1546) and Kircher.
115. Discovery of the thoracic duct. By Rudbeck (1651), Jolyff and Bertolinus (1653).

116. That the skull is made of modified vertebrae. By Goethe (1790) and Oken (1776).
117. Nature of the cataract. By Brisseau (1706) and Maitre-Jan (1707).
118. Operation for cure of aneurisms. By Hunter (1775) and Anil (1772).
119. Digestion as a chemical rather than a mechanical process. By Spallanzani and Hunter.
120. Function of the pancreas. By Purkinje (1836) and Pappenheim (1836).
121. Solution of the problem of respiration. By Priestley (1777), Scheele (1777), Lavoisier (1777), Spallanzani (1777) and Davy (1777).
122. Form of the liver cells. By Purkinje (1838), Heule (1838) and Dutrochet (1838).
123. Relation of micro-organisms to fermentation and putrefaction. By Latour (1837) and Schwann (1837).
124. Pepsin as the active principle of gastric juice. By Latour (1835) and Schwann (1835).
125. Prevention of putrefaction of wounds by keeping germs from surface of wound. By Lister (1867) and Guerin (1871).
126. Cellular basis of both animal and vegetable tissue. Claimed by Schwann (1839), Henle (1839?), Turpin (1839?), Dumortier (1839?), Purkinje (1839?), Muller (1839?) and Valentin (1839).
127. Invention of the laryngoscope. By Babington (1829), Liston (1737) and Garcia (1855).
128. Sulphuric ether as an anaesthetic. By Long (1842), Robinson (1846), Liston (1846), Morton (1846) and Jackson (1846).
129. That all appendages of a plant are modified leaves. By Goethe (1790) and Wolfe (1767).
130. Theory of inheritance of acquired characteristics. By E. Darwin (1794) and Lamarck (1801).
131. Theory of natural selection and variation. By C. Darwin (1858) and Wallace (1858).
132. Laws of heredity. By Mendel (1865), De Vries (1900), Correns (1900) and Tschermarck (1900).
133. Theory of mutations. By Korschinsky (1899) and De Vries (1900).
134. Theory of the emotions. By James (1884) and Lange (1887).
135. Theory of color. By Young (1801) and Helmholz.
136. Sewing machine. By Thimmonier (1830), Howe (1846) and Hunt (1840).

137. Balloon. By Montgolfier (1783), Rittenhouse-Hopkins (1783).
138. Flying machine. Claimed by Wright (1895-1901), Langley (1893-7) and others.
139. Reapers. By Hussey (1833) and McCormick (1834).
140. Doubly-flanged rail. By Stephens and Vignolet.
141. Steam boat. Claimed by Fulton (1807), Jouffroy, Rumsey, Stevens and Symmington (1802).
142. Printing. By Gutenberg (1443) and Coster (1420-23).
143. Cylinder printing press. By Koenig-Bensley (1812-13) and Napier (1830).
144. Typewriter. Claimed by Beach (1847-56), Sholes? (1872) and Wheatstone (1855-60).
145. Trolley car. By Van Doeple (1884-5), Sprague (1888), Siemens (1881) and Daft (1883).
146. Stereoscope. By Wheatstone (1839) and Elliott (1840).
147. Centrifugal pumps. By Appold (1850), Gwynne (1850) and Bessemer (1850).
148. Use of gasoline engines in automobiles. By Otto (1876), Daimler (1885) and Belden (1879?).

NOTES

[1]This statement is a conclusion based upon a study of the rate of evolution and the frequency of mutations. The researches are quite extensive and the limits of this paper do not permit a development of this point. [We now know, of course, that mutations occur at a very high rate. Nevertheless, the point raised by Ogburn and Thomas still stands. Neurological mutations affecting "intelligence" would require not a few generations—or even a few centuries—but many thousands of years to have an appreciable effect on human performance. In fact, anthropologists today assume that there has been no appreciable change in the mental abilities of the human species as a whole for at least the last 50,000 years.—[Eds.]

[2]Neither does it tell us *how* the synthesis of elements occurs in any particular case. To the best of our knowledge, the work of Homer G. Barnett is the only significant advance to date in this area. See Selection 1 of this volume, as well as Barnett's *Innovation* (1953). —Eds.]

Hiram Percy Maxim was an engineer, not a social scientist. He probably never learned of such contemporary figures as Plekhanov, Ogburn, or Kroeber; and he could not have known of culturology, which did not emerge for some years after Maxim published his memoirs in 1937. Yet, his personal account of his role in the invention of the automobile reveals a sophisticated grasp of the nature of culture as a supra-individual phenomenon and of the processes of cultural synthesis. For this reason, we have reprinted here the introductory chapter of his charming autobiography, Horseless Carriage Days, *which fortunately has been reissued recently in paperback (1962). Besides recommending a reading of the full account of Maxim's joys and struggles as an inventor of the automobile, we invite the student to use the excerpt reprinted here as a springboard for reflecting back on the preceding selections.*

One: 6

The Horseless Idea

*Hiram Percy Maxim**

Late one summer night in the year 1892, as I was pedaling my bicycle along a lonely road between Salem and Lynn in Massachusetts, the thought came to me that it would be a wonderful thing if a little engine were to be devised which would furnish the power to drive a bicycle. A little engine which would do what my legs were doing did not appear such a serious problem. I could not be expending more than a sixth or a quarter of a horsepower, and that would not mean much of an engine.

I had been spending the evening with an attractive young lady in Salem. I suspect that I was pretty much up in the clouds. At any rate, my thoughts were quickened on that lonely ride that night.

I thought about transportation. I saw it emerging from a crude stage in which mankind was limited to the railroad, to the horse, or to shank's mare. The bicycle was just becoming popular and it represented a very significant advance, I felt. Here I was covering the distance between Salem and Lynn on a bicycle. Here was a revolutionary change in transportation. My bicycle was propelled at a respectable speed by a mechanism operated by my muscles. It carried me over a lonely country road in the middle of the night, covering the distance in considerably less than an hour. A horse and carriage would require nearly two hours. A railroad train would require half an hour, and it would carry me only from station to station. And I must conform to its timetable, which was not always convenient when calling upon an attractive young lady in Salem.

If I could build a little engine and use its power to do the propelling, and if I could use a regular carriage instead of a bicycle, there would be

---

*"The Horseless Idea" from *Horseless Carriage Days* by Hiram Percy Maxim. Copyright 1936, 1937 by Harper & Row, Publishers. Reprinted by permission of the publishers. (Dover edition, 1962).

no limit to where I could go. Distances would be halved. Towns would become nearer together. More people would intermingle. It would profoundly influence the course of civilization itself. The idea seemed very worth while, as I pedaled along that lonely road that night. I fell to casting about in my mind for a suitable engine.

At this time I was superintendent of the American Projectile Company in Lynn. The company was a subsidiary of the Thomson Electric Welding Company, which was in turn a sort of a subsidiary of the Thomson-Houston Company, which later became the General Electric Company. Our American Projectile Company made projectiles for the army and navy by an electric welding process which had been developed by the late Lieut. William Maxwell Wood of the navy. Projectile-making was my vocation; but my avocation became searching for a suitable type of engine for driving a road vehicle.

Somebody had told me about an Otto gas-engine which was running a water-pump somewhere. I hastened to the place, and as I took my first look at a small gas-engine at work, I experienced a queer mixture of emotions. Was it the engine I was looking for? I had known about large gas-engines, but I had never seen one of these small engines at work. It had a slide valve, gas-jet ignition. This could easily be improved by using the hot-tube principle. It was upside down, the crank shaft being at the top of things; but this also could be fixed. The important matter was that it ran smoothly and sweetly. If gasoline were substituted for the illuminating gas on which the little engine was running, it seemed to be just what would be satisfactory on a vehicle. I was profoundly impressed as I lingered and watched that engine operate. I believed I was looking at the embryo of the engine of which I dreamed.

It must be remembered that I was young—in my early twenties. I hoped I might be the first to produce an engine-driven road vehicle, which was evidence of how young I was. This Otto engine proved that somebody, somewhere, had given a lot of time and thought to the small-engine problem. Was it likely he had overlooked its possibilities on a road vehicle? I had to face the cold fact that it was not. It was a horrid thought to a young fellow with my temperament. I consoled myself by thinking that, although somebody, somewhere, might have thought about using a gasoline-engine to drive a vehicle, nevertheless there were none of them running around on the roads. If I worked hard enough I yet might be first.

I was blissfully ignorant that Benz and Daimler in Germany; De Dion, Panhard, and a host of others in France; Napier and a few others in England; Duryea Brothers, Haynes, Apperson Brothers, Winton, and others in the United States—were working might and main on gasoline-propelled road vehicles. I was also blissfully ignorant of the existence of one George B. Selden of Rochester, New York, who had applied for a patent on my idea in the year 1877, when I was a little boy at school. As I look back, I am amazed that so many of us began work so nearly at the same time, and without the slightest notion that others were working on the problem. In 1892, when I began my work on a mechanical road vehicle, I suppose there were fifty persons in the United States working on the same idea.

Why did so many different and widely separated persons have the same thoughts at about the same time? In my case the idea came from looking down and contemplating the mechanism of my legs and the bicycle cranks while riding along a lonely road in the middle of the night. I suppose not another one of us pioneers had his original inspiration come to him as mine came to me. Probably every one of us acquired his original conception from an entirely different set of circumstances resulting from accidental conditions.

It has always been my belief that we all began to work on the gasoline-engine-propelled road vehicle at about the same time because it had become apparent that civilization was ready for the mechanical vehicle. It was natural that this idea should strike many of us at about the same time. It has been the habit to give the gasoline-engine all the credit for bringing the automobile, as we term the mechanical road vehicle today. In my opinion this is a wrong explanation. We have had the steam-engine for over a century. We could have built steam vehicles in 1880, or indeed in 1870. But we did not. We waited until 1895.

The reason why we did not build mechanical road vehicles before this, in my opinion, was because the bicycle had not yet come in numbers and had not directed men's minds to the possibilities of independent, long-distance travel over the ordinary highway. We thought the railroad was good enough. The bicycle created a new demand which it was beyond the ability of the railroad to supply. Then it came about that the bicycle could not satisfy the demand which it had created. A mechanically propelled vehicle was wanted instead of a foot-propelled one, and we now know that the automobile was the answer.

Since the last word has by no means been said in transportation, what is likely to be the tendency from here on? The automobile demand had to come before a reliable gasoline-engine could be developed. When this engine became available the airplane appeared. The airplane has arrived at a stage where it is one of our established systems of transportation. This brings us to the interesting question, what is it whose coming has had to await the airplane? I suspect it is an entirely new form of motive power. The airplane has created a demand for something beyond the ability of the gasoline-engine to supply. This something is bound to appear. Who shall say that another fifty forward-looking men are not at work independently upon it at this moment, keeping their efforts secret just as we horseless-carriage pioneers forty years ago kept our efforts secret, and just as blissfully ignorant of one another's existence as we were? History has a strange way of repeating itself.

PART TWO

The Prime-Mover of

Cultural Evolution

The search for a single force, or prime-mover, underlying cultural evolution is very old. Perhaps the major reason why so much energy has been expended in this pursuit is that the discovery of a single force would lend conceptual unity and elegance to the study of human society and culture. In this essay, Elman Service argues against all previous monistic theories and raises serious doubts as to whether a single force will ever be discovered.

Because the essay was written in part as a reaction to Marvin Harris' The Rise of Anthropological Theory *(1968)*, Harris' spirited rebuttal, "Monistic Determinism: Anti-Service" *(1969)*, should be consulted. We also recommend Marshall Sahlins and Elman Service's Evolution and Culture *(1960)*, and especially Service's essay therein, "The Law of Evolutionary Potential" *(pp. 93-122; B-M, A-206; also available in Service 1971:31-49; for a self-criticism, see Service 1969:71-72)*. Other appropriate and readily available materials include Sir Julian Huxley's "Evolution, Cultural and Biological" *(1955; B-M, A-123)* and Leslie White's "Energy and the Evolution of Culture" *(1949:363-393; B-M, A-235)*.

Two: 1

The Prime-Mover of Cultural Evolution

Elman R. Service*

The main burden of this article has been presented in talks to student clubs during the past two years. The purpose was to argue against the widespread notion that a theory of cultural evolution necessarily involves a monistic determinism, a "prime-mover" of some sort. The recent publication of Harris' *The Rise of Anthropological Theory* (1968) has made it timely to present the argument to a wider audience.

Harris has reviewed anthropological thought since its beginnings in the Enlightenment and graded the various theories primarily in terms of their degree of departure from what he considers the source of cultural change, techno-economic determinism. Many of his criticisms of other theories are well-taken, and I have borrowed them freely in several instances. (There are several inaccurate accounts and mistaken judgments, too; but since this is not a review, I shall not refer to them further.)

It is convenient to list the main currents in the history of thought about cultural evolution in terms of competing theories about the determinants of evolutionm ooxne nennotn on nkrse, do justice to all of them in a single article, but that is not the point: I think it is important to establish that there is a way of thinking about evolution that permits an openness about the locus of causality. Another way to put it is that most of the prime-mover arguments are each probably somewhat, or sometimes, right. This is not an expression of indeterminism, however, but only a statement that the acceptance of one prime-mover to the exclusion of others inhibits what should be an empirical study of the locus of causality.

*Reprinted with the permission of the author and publisher from *Southwestern Journal of Anthropology*, Vol. 24, Winter 1968, pp. 396-409.

Elman R. Service is professor of anthropology at the University of California at Santa Barbara.

According to Webster, *prime-mover* used figuratively means simply "the original or most effective force in any understanding." It is important to stipulate, however, that for the prime-mover to account for evolutionary change, which of course is variable, the prime-mover must be itself a variable. Hence, it is not synonymous with something "basic" or "important," since such aspects of life and culture might be constants like matter and energy, or physical and psychic needs.

It should be understood also that only the prime-movers that are scientifically arguable will be discussed, to the exclusion of theological, mystical, or metaphysical theories. Thus we may agree with Harris to ignore theories like those of Rousseau and some others of his day who made a prime-mover out of the "general will," which created as well as legitimized political organizations. In sad fact, much as we must admire the grand efflorescence of evolutionary thought in 18th century France, the typical propensity to depend on verbalisms like "natural law" and "general will" as explanatory devices must be regarded as both mystical and tautological. (This may seem like too high-handed a dismissal, so I hasten to add that we shall return to the Enlightenment philosophers later for a consideration of several other aspects of their thought.)

Racistic and biologistic theories of cultural evolution have always been with us, mostly in the public domain, but they have been so thoroughly demolished for so long in anthropology that they will not be discussed here.

Geographical determinism of various kinds has a long history, from the classical Greeks through the 14th century Ibn Khaldun, 16th century Jean Bodin, to the 18th century Enlightenment philosophers. But these thinkers need not concern us since they did not address themselves to cultural evolutionary stages, but only to national or racial psychological characteristics. Of the later philosophers, Montesquieu came the closest to a scientific appreciation of the influence of geographical conditions on culture. But his *L'Esprit des Lois* was concerned primarily with the relationship of a nation's legal system to natural conditions of climate and soil. This is not a theory of the determinants of evolutionary change; like most of his contemporaries, Montesquieu believed the ultimate prime-mover to be mentality. In the end this is, as Harris points out, indeterministic idealism, neatly spelled out by Montesquieu himself: "It is in the nature of human laws to be subject to all the accidents which can happen, and to vary in proportion as the will of man changes" (Harris 1968:21).

Even the modern anthropogeography developed at the University of California (Berkeley) was not related to a theory of evolutionary change. To Sauer and Kroeber, the main proponents of this approach, geographical variables importantly channel cultural changes, to be sure. But change itself remains vague; it is referred to as "history," "diffusion," "drift," and the unfolding of "pattern" (Kroeber 1939). This is not the approach of determinism, nor even a theory of change. The greatest relevance of the anthropogeographical school to cultural evolutionism is that it fostered the development of the "multilinear" theory of Steward,[1] who had been a graduate student of Kroeber's.

Major Prime-Movers

Cultural evolutionism was the major preoccupation of important philosophers of the 18th century in France and Britain. To be sure, others had much earlier referred to evolution and even proposed grand schemes, like the universal theory of Lucretius, but the matter of its determinants did not come importantly into focus.

The question of specific determinants begins, of course, with the very question of determinism itself, and this has always been perplexing. Most of the 18th century evolutionists, it is true, cited "natural laws" as often and as easily as their predecessors had spoken of "God's will," yet at the same time they believed that the gradual unfolding of superior cultural institutions was a consequence of improvements in human reasoning. We shall have to discuss at some length this paradoxical blend of determinism and free-will that characterizes much of evolutionary thought from the 18th century to this very day. One of the major purposes of this essay is to lay the problem to rest.

Mentalistic Idealism

The modifier *mentalistic* is used here to broaden the scope of the discussion, particularly in order to distinguish the present subject from the more narrow and clearcut idealism of a Hegel. By mentalism, I mean simply that since every cultural custom or institution has its subjective aspect—since it exists in some form in the mind as well as concretely, objectively, or behaviorally—it is natural enough for some to think of the subjective as underlying the objective and, thus, as prior to it in some sense. It is obvious that the human ability to think and communicate in ways that no other animal can is the prerequisite that enables human behavior to be so distinct in salient ways, to become *cultural* behavior. The mental aspect truly is of great significance, and this has led to the long-standing and widespread propensity to consider mind as the determinant of human behavior and hence as the locus of explanations of differences in the forms culture may take.

The most prominent manifestations of mentalistic explanations appeared, appropriately enough, in France during the so-called Age of Reason. Modern savages and our primitive ancestors, thought the *philosophes,* lived in a "state of nature." Civilization was achieved in proportion to the increase in rational thought—civilized man had literally thought himself out of savagery. Since this is conscious and intentful thought, it was not, strictly speaking, considered a form of determinism: *conscious* mentation equals free-will, hence the indeterminism of human institutions, which "vary in proportion as the will of man changes" (Harris 1968:21).

Morgan, one of the most important pioneers of modern anthropology, reveals the same contradictory mixture of determinism and free-will, though in rather more complicated form than the above description. Morgan saw evolution in two separate aspects: inventions and discoveries "stand to each other in progressive relations," while social institutions are in "unfolding relations." "While the former class have had a connection, more or less direct, the latter have been developed from a few primary germs of thought" (Morgan 1963:4). Since *Ancient Society* is almost wholly devoted to the "unfolding" evolution of such institutions as the family, tribe, and state, it must be considered that its main thrust is essentially in support of mentalistic-idealistic determinants of evolution. (The major subdivisions of the book are titled, *Growth of the Idea of the Family, Growth of the Idea of Government,* etc.) Late in the book, however, Morgan introduced an important deterministic note which will be discussed more fully below in the section, *"The Technological Imperative."*

A similar blend of determinism with free will is characteristic of Marxism. Technology and its related socio-economic functions have determined the course of evolution in the past, but "with the seizing of the means of production by society, production of commodities and, simultaneously, the mastery of the product over the producer are abolished." As man, armed with the proper revolutionary understanding of history, consciously begins to make his own history, he ascends "from the kingdom of necessity to the kingdom of freedom" (Engels 1961:80-81).

This theory-that-sets-us-free is, of course, most evident in modern times in the religious fervor with which Russian and Chinese Communists argue about "revisionism" and "Mao's thoughts," and so on, with respect to the sacred texts of Marx and Engels. As in the case of the Enlightenment theorists, this argument is related to the implicit but basic assumption that evolution is determined by external forces when people are unaware, and that it is made free, undetermined, when their awareness begins. (This will be discussed as a mistake in scientific logic in later pages.)

Another but rather different version of mentalism has lately visited anthropology. It is new and different in that it proposes that there is an *unconscious* structure of mentation that underlies social and cultural institutions, rather than the above conscious rationalism. This is the influence of structural linguistics as reflected in the ideas of Lévi-Strauss and in the methodology termed "componential analysis." In the latter case, unconscious thought is not proposed as a determinant of evolution; these analysts are only applying a simple method to some minor aspects of culture that are largely linguistic—they are not explaining anything. Even when they claim to have discovered some unconscious forms of "cognition," they have remained merely descriptive, not explanatory. So far no particular harm is done, except to take up time and space.[2] But great violence is done to the rules of scientific logic when any imagined "cognitive processes" or Lévi-Strauss' "structure" of mentation are used as *explanations* of the cultural phenomena at issue. I do not know that any componential analysts have ever committed such blatant tautologies, but it would be easy to do so, and for that reason it is worth calling attention to the danger.

But in the case of Lévi-Strauss the circularity is glaringly plain. Cultural institutions and customs provide data from which unconscious logico-mathematical laws of mentation are *inferred* by him (for, of course, they cannot be observed); and afterwards these universal mental laws will "explain" human culture in all its many forms.[3]

The fact that mentalistic idealism has plagued the social sciences from the 18th century to this very day means that there is something remarkably beguiling about it, since it has persisted despite the obviousness of its utter lack of fruitfulness for all that time. It must, therefore, be discussed critically in this section before proceeding to the more wholesome pleasure of sorting out the virtues that the other prime-movers exhibit.

That the new mentalism refers to unconscious forms of cognition and logical structures of thought rather than to the intellection that Enlightenment theorists assumed was the cultural prime-mover does not save it from exactly the same scientific criticisms. Any explanation of cultural institutions by resort to mentation, conscious or not, will exhibit at least three logical fallacies—any one of which renders it useless. These fallacies are that the explanation is untestable, tautological, and reductionistic.

Untestability simply means that mentalistic explanations are only guesses that must go forever unproved. Since the mental factors cannot be observed, there is absolutely no way to add factual support to the mentalistic assertion, and this means, of course, that it is a metaphysical and not a scientific proposition.

Mentalistic idealism is *tautological* in the sense that the posited mental aspect, which cannot be observed, is inferred from the cultural phenomenon that is observed; when that inference, in turn, becomes the *explanation* of the cultural institution, a perfect circle, however freehand, has been drawn.

The *reductionism* is simply the obvious, though very common, fallacy of trying to explain the specific in terms of the general—variables in terms of constants. The questions at issue have to do with explanations of cultural variations, with the causes of the evolutionary changes that result in different cultural stages. Any explanation that uses underlying general biological, psychological, or mental characteristics could help explain (if it did) only pan-human, universal cultural characteristics.[4] If the mental characteristics are not pan-human, but are different in proportion to the differences in the cultural institutions (which they would have to be if they explained the cultural differences), then what? Are we back to racism?

The most general, the most profound, and the most important conclusion that anthropology has to offer the world is simply this: whereas individuals may differ in their innate bio-psychological (or "mental," if you like) makeup, races, national populations, and above all, the great and heterogeneous populations within cultural stages could not possibly differ enough in their genetic makeup to explain the great differences in their respective cultures. It is hard to see how any modern would-be anthropologist, like Lévi-Strauss, can be forgiven for violating an anthropological conclusion that is so well established as to be nowadays axiomatic.

The striking reductionism of modern mentalistic idealism is precisely the same as the ancient fallacy exhibited by the *philosophes*. Harris, in criticizing the 18th century evolutionists, put it this way (1968:39):

> A few preliminary comments concerning the problems that an emphasis upon "mind" and "reason" present to the theory-

building endeavors of cultural anthropology are needed at this point. Let us agree that scientific explanations are statements of the conditions under which predicted or retrodicted events will occur. To explain sociocultural differences and similarities exclusively in terms of more or less reasonable thought and action is to omit any statement of conditions. In the view of many eighteenth-century social philosophers, the explanation of why the Iroquois did not behave like Frenchmen was the Indians' self-imposed failure to think their way far enough out of the state of nature. But under what conditions will a group think themselves into bilaterality rather than matrilaterality, monogamy rather than polygamy, private property rather than communal ownership, etc.? Unless such conditions are specified, appeal to the effects of rational inventiveness serves merely to obscure an enduring ignorance of scientifically admissible explanations.

This form of mentalism is very different from the above-mentioned theory-that-sets-us-free form of idealism and is much more plainly fallacious. In Marxist idealism the prime-moving power resides in the quality of an ideology, the visible products of mentation, but not unobservable mentation itself. This prime-mover has a curious and interesting history and is worth discussing at length, in another context, for its importance as a cultural process. But its significance as a theory, however, is in political weaponry; it has had little or no influence in Western social science. (Marxism in the form of techno-economic determinism has had a tremendous influence, of course, but here we are discussing the opposite side of the coin, its indeterministic idealism.)

Is there anything at all defensible about the feeling many of us have that a "good" or "right" theory can somehow free us from the "Kingdom of Necessity" to better master our civilizational course? Could a theory play a causal, instrumental, even technical, role in history? If the reader is a social scientist interested in theory, as is the present writer, then we probably agree that our attempts to improve theory ought to be based on the assumption that it will do some good. An evolutionary theory, for example, that could predict the economic and political behavior of the Far East, even if only at very long range, would be immensely valuable. This is not an argument about the likelihood of such a splendid theory soon appearing, but only to consider the proposition that *if* such a theory were to appear, *could* it have some useful effects? So far our truths have been more beautiful than useful, but we have—have we not?—exerted at least a little political leverage via critical knowledge of such things as the U.S.A.'s Vietnam blunder.

Conflict Theories

The theory that conflict and competition result in improvement is, of course, very widespread in this general vague form. More specific and more famous in the history of evolutionary thought are the theorists who argued that conflict was directly responsible for the transition from tribal society to state society and for subsequent improvements that lay at the very origin of civilization. The theories are of two distinguishable kinds: those that emphasize the role of conflict among groups and persons *within* a society, and those that emphasize conflict *among* societies. Thomas Hobbes, David Hume, and Adam Ferguson are perhaps the most influential protagonists of the first approach, while the latter is best represented by Herbert Spencer, Walter Bagehot, Ludwig Gumplowicz, and Franz Oppenheimer.

Certainly one of the obvious functions of the legal edifice we call the state is the preservation of internal public order, the reduction of and channeling of conflict and competition. It does not follow, of course, that an important function of an institution is its explanation, nor that the function is responsible for its genesis, but the rise of the state surely has something to do with the rise of competition. It remains difficult to see how these theorists can be gainsaid, out of hand, without a great deal more effort than has been expended in research on this topic so far.

But those who have also stressed conflict among whole societies have had one important advantage; this theory can simultaneously account for both aspects of stateness—the rise of its domestic *and* foreign political functions.

The above idea was cogently promulgated by Bagehot (1873), the first avowed Social Darwinist, who was an important influence on Spencer's political ideas. Primitive societies that are superior in warfare, he thought, are likely to have superior law, centralized leadership, and, most importantly, a system of peaceful succession to positions of leadership. These are all, of course, related to social stability, and Bagehot laid special stress on this aspect of polity. To be sure, a technological and military superiority may account for the ascendency of some particular society over another at any given time, but this can only be temporary. Over the long run, superior governmental devices are necessary to maintain the ascendency. Highly motivated, brave, and ferocious armies, such as the Vandals, Huns, or Mongols therefore could win only ephemeral victories, for over time, as Bagehot states, "the tamest are the strongest."

It should be of interest that of the much longer list of conflict theorists that could be compiled, there seems to be no evolutionary anthropologist who was Darwinistic with respect to either internal or external competition as the source of societal or political evolution. In other words, there never was the "biological analogy" of Social Darwinism in anthropology that the Boasian anthropologists fought against so valiantly. The only analogy from biology was the *organismic* ("structural-functional") model developed by Radcliffe-Brown from one aspect of Durkheim's many-sided and confusing philosophy. But there is nowhere in any of the writing of the functionalists a hint of Darwinism, nor for that matter of any other determinants of evolution (except for a reference to the role of the "struggle for existence" by Durkheim himself).[5]

Marxists are often included among the various kinds of conflict theorists. But Marx's "class struggle" is actually a precipitation out of techno-economic evolution. Despite its significance as a catalyst of revolution it is not a prime-mover in evolution: it remains as the aforementioned theory-that-sets-us-free and technology.

The Technological Imperative

When Adam Ferguson and Turgot described the Hunting, Pastoralism, and Farming stages of evolution, they also introduced an explicit, though very general, idea of the evolutionary significance of technology. A hunting technology has obvious social and economic functional correlates. With the advent of herding, and later of full farming, a people's way of life is fundamentally changed. But neither of these writers, nor Montesquieu, with his closely related stages of Savagery, Barbarism, and Civilization, developed the theory much beyond this general conception.

Morgan was the first to add greater specificity. To be sure, most of his master work, *Ancient Society*, retained the mentalistic approach of the previous century, but late in the book Morgan presented the argument that when, in the course of evolution, the production of goods became so prolific that private trade and property became prevalent, then the family, society, and the state would be altered. Morgan's idea was of tremendous significance in the history of evolutionary thought, for it was the catalyst of the more fully realized technological imperative of Marx and Engels.

Marx and Engels borrowed directly and generously from *Ancient Society,* but they emphasized particularly the above theory of the technological genesis of property in what finally became the classic book of Engels: *The Origin of the Family, Private Property, and the State* (1942). In the evolution of society, technological improvements led to increasing amounts of goods, with consequent greater trade, commodity production, and private property, followed by an economic division of the society into rich and poor, workers and capitalists. The state arises as a device to protect this nascent capitalism from the exploited poor. Even religion changes its character in order to justify this order of society. Thus the functional changes are, in turn: technology →economy →polity →ideology.

Marxism was the first theory that consistently connected techno-economic evolution to the other major aspects of culture. Put another way, this was the first time that structural-functional, parts-to-the-whole relationships were envisaged.

But just as in Morgan's case, the 18th century mentalistic legacy remains. The impersonal determinants of evolution are overcome by the freedom of human beings to change the system—if they have the right theory.

Sometimes one of the material consequences of technology, such as a surplus of food, is cited as of the greatest priority. Engels put it this way: ". . . mankind must first of all eat and drink, have shelter and clothing, before it can pursue politics, science, religion, art, etc." (Engels 1883:16). Childe's *Man Makes Himself* is probably the best-known anthropological work that used the economic surplus as prime-mover.

Sometimes "leisure," as a concomitant of surplus food production, is cited as the immediate causal factor in evolution. Boas (1940:285) expressed the idea in this manner: ". . . a surplus of food supply is liable to bring about an increase of population and an increase of leisure, which gives opportunity for occupations that are not absolutely necessary for the needs of everyday life."

White has developed the most specifically monistic and the most general application of a theory of technological determinants to sources of energy. He writes: "Culture advances as the amount of energy harnessed per capita per year increases, or as the efficiency or economy of the means of controlling energy is increased, or both" (1959b:56). White's view of technology as the creator of harnessed energy and thus as the prime-mover of cultural advance should be understood as related to a view of the evolution of world culture as an interrelated whole. He is, of course, well aware that the cultures of particular societies develop and diverge in idiosyncratic ways, with technology, however important, as one variable among many. Taking the culture of mankind as a whole, nevertheless, it would appear that the grandest stages of development can be appropriately demarked by technological innovations such as plant and animal domestication, irrigation agriculture, fueled engines, and the like. Many anthropologists would acknowledge this but wonder what is the further use of the formula. If technology is the prime-mover, then it ought to be useful in explaining the evolution of actual, specific societies. The formula obviously would apply to the great Industrial Revolution of Western Europe and to many other areas influenced by it. But this would be to maintain, in effect, that where technological changes occurred that were important, we should regard them as important. Who would argue with that?

But technology as *prime-mover* in a formula must mean something more. In the Marxian example of the theory, technology is the key that unlocks and reveals how *all* societies work. The special purpose of the theory, of course, was to predict the time and place of the breakdown of industrial capitalism. And, logically, the fact that it has so dramatically failed to do this is the positive proof that it is wrong. The reason that Marxism nevertheless remains as official dogma in such a large part of the world lies in its politico-ideological and quasi-religious significance as a creed rather than in its original intellectual significance.

White is also very different from Morgan and the Marxists in recognizing the determinism-freedom paradox and facing it squarely. The science of culture, or culturology, as he calls it, is a way of looking at human behavior as if it were completely determined by its cultural matrix and thus explainable by scientific investigation. The key is *as if.* The question of the ontological reality of cultural determinism in human affairs is not faced, in the philosophical sense, simply because there is no way of solving it—except, of course, with metaphysical pronouncements. But one way of handling problems about human behavior is to put them *in the context of* scientific determinism.[6] The test thus becomes simply whether or not our comprehension is increased. If it is, even slightly, then the deterministic approach is better than nothing—i.e., better than indeterminism. On the other hand, if one wishes to exhort the "masses," foment the class struggle, or get out the vote, he may find it psychologically, if not intellectually, necessary to believe in his free will. But this is different from an attempt at scientific *understanding* of the behavior. As for understanding, even the very belief in free will could be analyzed deterministically, as an aspect of culture; its provenience, history, and its functional connection to other aspects of culture could be studied.

Conclusion

Down with prime-movers! There is no single magical formula that will predict the evolution of every society. The actual evolution of the culture of particular societies is an adaptive process whereby the society solves problems with respect to the natural and to the human-competitive environment. These environments are so diverse, the problems so numerous, and the solutions potentially so various that no single determinant can be equally powerful for all cases.

To be sure, some kind of technological production of necessities, especially of food, is required for any society. In the context of evolution, such production is an *enabler*, so to speak, without which an increase in size and density could not take place. But a necessity or enabler is not necessarily a mover. Many stabilized societies could produce much more than they do, but it does not follow that they necessarily will, nor that if they did that they would necessarily "evolve" in some sense.[7]

To say that "problems are solved" in the adaptive process is a figure of speech, and possibly a misleading one. I do not mean to imply that the problems are likely to be intellectually posed and solved. Adaptation is problem-solving only in a very general sense, and furthermore it seems likely that it is only we, looking back in history or at a primitive society, rather than the participants, who can recognize the problems and the solutions and describe them in intellectual terms. Yet, on the other hand, there are some problems—usually political ones—that are sometimes capable of creative, rational solutions. And it is these that loom so large today and for which we need theories of evolution that can give us some guidance (and "freedom") for purposeful action.

But the question of what is prime-mover in any case of specific evolutionary change is an empirical question, the answer not to be found in advance of research by commitment to a specific theory of prime-movers. Similarly, whether the adaptive solutions were produced by intellectual effort and choice from among alternatives or were functional adjustments unintended by anyone in the society is also a factual question, though usually difficult to answer for lack of evidence.

It seems necessary to make this point because, as mentioned earlier, many people seem to think that determinism in social or cultural behavior is a product of the people's unawareness, while freedom is associated with awareness—that conscious progress is free progress. But this relationship bothers some people. Are you a determinist or aren't you? Make up your mind. A simple error in logic, however, is the cause of this discomfort.

Determinism is a perspective that a scientist takes up for the purposes of his investigation, just as arbitrarily as an astronomer decides to use his telescope. In contrast to the prime-mover problem, which should be decided empirically, the question is not whether or not determinism exists in nature. It is a point of view which, like a telescope, should be used in a certain way for certain investigations simply because it works. It cannot be fruitfully argued as something that is empirically true or false.

Reprise:

Could technology be *sometimes* a determiner of evolutionary changes in certain other aspects of culture? Yes.

Could competition or conflict among individuals be *sometimes...*? Yes.

Could competition or conflict among societies be *sometimes . . .*? Yes.

Could consciously formed social and political schemes and plans be *sometimes . . .*? Yes.

Are there unconscious "structures" of human thought and cognition that *sometimes . . .*? Nobody knows.

NOTES

[1]Steward is not inclined to causal monism, except for sometimes referring to techno-economic aspects of culture as "primary" in the adaptive relation to geographic condi-

tions. The present article therefore does not find further occasion to refer to his work. He may be the only important evolutionist who has not committed himself to any particular prime-mover.

[2]No particular good is done either. Few anthropologists are persuaded that either Lévi-Strauss or the componential analysts have showed us anything at all about the human mind. For critiques see Burling (1964) and Berreman (1966).

[3]See especially his collection of programmatic essays (Lévi-Strauss 1963).

[4]Consider this remarkable statement by Lévi-Strauss: "In anthropology as in linguistics, therefore, it is not comparison that supports generalization, but the other way around. If, as we believe to be the case, the unconscious activity of the mind consists in imposing forms upon content, and if these forms are fundamentally the same for all minds—ancient and modern, primitive and civilized . . .—it is necessary and sufficient to grasp the unconscious structure underlying each institution and each custom, in order to obtain a principle of interpretation valid for other institutions and other customs, provided of course that the analysis is carried far enough" (1963:21). Or, as he states elsewhere ". . . understanding consists in the reduction of one level of reality to another; that true reality is never the more obvious of realities . . ." (1964:61).

[5]Briefly paraphrased: The division of labor in society is increased as it becomes more voluminous and dense because then the struggle for existence is more acute. The more points of contact that individuals have, the more they are exposed to conflict—unless they specialize (Durkheim 1933:266-269).

[6]White's best exposition of this point is his article "The Concept of Culture" (1959a).

[7]Carneiro (1961) cogently disposed of this matter of food production as a determinant of evolution in his analysis of Kuikuru slash-and-burn cultivation.

For the first two million years or so of his existence, man was exclusively a hunter and gatherer. Not until some 10-15,000 years ago in the Old World, and some 7-9,000 years ago in the New World, did man become a food producer, rather than merely a predator on wild resources. The eventual effects of this change of subsistence base on the growth of culture were so great that anthropologists speak of the period of initial domestication of plants as the "Agricultural Revolution."

Why did the domestication of plants occur so recently in man's history? How did it occur? Why did agriculture originate in some places, such as the Near East and the Valley of Mexico, but not in others? The following essay by Leslie A. White provides a thoughtful framework for investigating these and related questions.

The student who wishes to pursue the specifics of agricultural origins and early consequences should consult Adams (1962; B-M, A-254), Braidwood and Reed (1957; B-M, A-23), Flannery (1965; B-M, A-415), Harlan (1971), Mangelsdorf (1958; B-M, A-153), Mangelsdorf et al. (1964; B-M, A-365), Reed (1959; B-M, A-188), and Solheim (1972).

Two: 2

The Agricultural Revolution

Leslie A. White*

Agriculture was not the result of a single discovery or invention. The theory that "the idea" of the cultivation of plants suddenly flashed across the mind of some man or woman long ago, evoked perhaps by the discovery that seeds thrown away from a meal had subsequently sprouted, and that the whole complex of agricultural techniques and practices grew out of this "idea," is simple and naive. It is, of course, but an example of the anthropomorphic and psychologistic type of explanation of culture that has so long characterized the reflections of the folk and the layman. According to this point of view, to explain an element of culture, all you have to do is to invoke a hypothetical individual who first "got the idea" of the trait in question; the trait is regarded as the external expression of the idea. If an invention or discovery did not take place, it was because no one "had the idea." The sterility of such reasoning is obvious. Events are "explained" in terms of ideas. But the occurrence or nonoccurrence of ideas is not explained at all.

We are not to think of the origin of agriculture as due to the chance discovery that seeds thrown away from a meal subsequently sprouted. Mankind knew all this and more for tens of thousands of years before the cultivation of plants began. We know that primitive peoples of modern times, wholly without agriculture, have nevertheless an abundant and accurate knowledge of the flora of their habitats. They know that seeds sprout, that parched plants are revived by rain, that they grow better in one soil than another, etc. No tribe of the modern world, however primitive, is without a vast amount of realistic knowledge and

*From *The Evolution of Culture* by Leslie A. White, pp. 283-289. Copyright © 1959 by McGraw-Hill, Inc. Used with permission of the author and McGraw-Hill Book Company.

Leslie A. White, who taught at the University of Michigan for more than thirty years, is currently research anthropologist at the University of California at Santa Barbara.

understanding of the nature and behavior of plants in their locality, and we may therefore infer that prehistoric man, long before the origin of agriculture, possessed a like knowledge of his flora. The origin of agriculture was not, therfore, the result of an idea or discovery; the cultivation of plants required no new facts or knowledge. Agriculture was simply a new kind of relationship between man—or more properly, woman—and plants.

All peoples use plant materials in one way or another. Man's prehuman ancestors undoubtedly subsisted in part, perhaps largely, upon plant foods, and it is a sound inference that all peoples, during the hundreds of thousands of years of human history, have used plants for food and also for other purposes. Even a people like the modern Eskimo, who subsist largely upon meat, nevertheless eat berries, leaves, lichens, etc., even salvaging plant material from the intestines of slain caribou for their mess.

We have, then, an intimate association between man and the flora of his habitat throughout the entire length of human history. And this intimate association meant knowledge and understanding of plants on man's part, as we have just indicated. At the outset of his career as a human being man was exploiting the wild-plant resources of his habitat, just as his anthropoïd ancestors had done before him. Various tools and techniques were devised and developed for this purpose. Innumerable cultural systems have been quite capable of providing the human beings within their embrace with an adequate supply of food derived wholly from wild flora and fauna. Cultural systems relate man to habitat, and an equilibrium can be established in this relationship as in others. When an equilibrium has been established culturally between man and habitat, it may be continued indefinitely, until it is upset by the intrusion of a new factor, the disappearance of an old one, or a radical change in the cultural configuration. Agriculture began when the old equilibrium of hunting and gathering was upset, and a new type of adjustment, a new kind of relationship to local flora, became requisite to survival.

We have no adequate records of how, when, and where this new type of adjustment became necessary and took place. We do know, however, that man's whole relationship with plants involves two significant factors: human effort, or labor, on the one hand, and plant materials capable of serving human needs and obtained by the expenditure of human energy, on the other. There is a ratio E:P between the expenditure of human energy and plant product. In the gathering of wild-plant food so many ergs of human energy are expended and so many calories of food are obtained. If natural resources are abundant, the amount of food obtained per unit of human energy expended will be large; if they are meager, the return will be small, the technological factor being constant.

In order to continue to exist, man must obtain from his efforts at least as much energy in the form of food as he has expended in putting forth these efforts; should he receive less he will eventually die of starvation. It is of course desirable from the standpoint of security and survival to obtain considerably more energy in the form of food than was expended in obtaining it. There have been, as we know, many cultural systems that have been able to make life secure for its human occupants by exploiting the wild-food resources of their respective habitats. Many have been able to do much more than to supply the bare necessities of life; they have provided surpluses which have made a considerable amount of art, ceremony, and recreation possible. Even very crude cultures like those of aboriginal Australia were able to do this.

But suppose the relationship between man and his wild-plant food supply undergoes change adversely to man. Population pressure upon food supply may be increased by immigration. Or the food supply may decrease as a consequence of meteorologic or physiographic change. In either case, the amount of food per capita per square mile will decrease if the technological factor remains constant. This will mean a decrease of amount of food produced per unit of human energy expended. If food is scarce in one's immediate vicinity, he may make up for the deficiency by foraging farther afield, but this requires more effort, more energy.

It may happen, therefore, that the amount of food obtained per unit of human energy expended may be diminished from one cause or another. When this occurs one or another of the following consequences must follow: (1) a lower standard of living, or, to express it in other words, cultural regression, (2) emigration, or (3) agriculture or animal husbandry or both.

In analyzing the energy relationship between man and plants— energy expended, plant food obtained—we must consider not only the amount of energy expended in human labor but the way in which it is expended as well. Gathering wild plant food is one way of expending human energy in food production; agriculture is another. *Agriculture* is merely the name we give to various ways of increasing man's control over the lives of plants. And the significant thing about this increase in control is that it may increase the amount of food produced per unit of human labor. The farmer with well-developed agricultural techniques can produce more food per unit of human energy expended, or better, per man-year, than can the gatherer of wild plant food in all but the most abundant of wild resources.

At certain times and places in the course of culture history, the threat of a diminished food supply, coming from an increase of population pressure through immigration, or from a decline in local flora due to climatic or physiographic change, was met by various measures of cultural control over plant life, which, collectively, we call agriculture.

We are still faced with such questions as, "Why did agriculture begin, in the Old World, about 8000 B.C. rather than 50,000?" and "Why did it begin where it did rather than in other places?" These are questions of specific fact rather than problems of general theory, and we do not have enough facts to answer them at present. We must suppose that a certain degree of cultural development is necessary for the inauguration of an agricultural technology; we would not expect that a cultural system only 50,000 or 100,000 years above an anthropoid level could launch an agricultural way of life. But we can see no reason why cultural systems of 50,00 B.C. (i.e. , 950,000 years old) could not have been capable of originating agriculture as well as systems in 8000 B.C. (990, 000 years old). We must look, then, to environmental—climatic and physiographic—factors and to the possibility of population movements, rather than to cultural factors, for the answers to these questions.

Childe and the Braidwoods have suggested that climatic change at the close of the last great Ice Age in the Old World, with its consequent changes in flora and fauna, affected cultural systems and set the stage for agriculture and animal husbandry, if it did not actually initiate these arts.[1] According to their theory, great areas of central Asia became desiccated after the retreat of the ice sheet—and there appears to be geologic evidence of this—causing their inhabitants to migrate to more suitable habitats. This migration increased the population, and consequently the pressure upon food supply, in the areas in which the migrants settled. The increased pressure upon food supply upset the equilibrium between need and supply, initiating attempts to *control* food supply through the use of new techniques—as well as, perhaps, the refinement or extension of old ones—to control the growth and reproduction of plants. This is agriculture.

Agriculture, then, is a matter of cultural control over the lives of plant species. And this control was not a matter of all or none, but a matter of kind and degree. We can observe beginnings of such control among many cultures usually—and quite properly—designated as non-agricultural.

First of all, no doubt, were the magical attempts at control. The totemic ceremonies of aboriginal tribes of Australia well exemplify this attempt to control the lives of certain plant and animal species and to increase the food supply thereby. Eventually, and at first sporadically and little by little, came rational attempts at control. Seeds might be sown, and then left to themselves: many tribes of the Great Lakes region in North America used to sow wild rice in marshes to increase the yield, but did nothing else until the harvest. Some wild plants were tended to help them in their struggle with nature. Irrigation preceded agriculture in some regions (cf. Steward 1930:149-156). The first agriculture was nomadic, so to speak, in some instances. Seeds would be sown in the spring before leaving the winter encampment for the summer's hunt or grazing. Upon returning in the fall the crops, if any remained, would be harvested.

Increased concern with plant growth, more control over their way of life, resulted in increased yields. Labor spent in this way came to be more profitable, more lucrative, than effort confined to gathering natural produce only. Control became deliberate and systematic. New techniques were developed, and new tools invented. More and more plants, for textiles, drugs, and liquors, as well as for food, were domesticated. The best seeds were used for planting. Competing plants were eliminated or restricted by hoeing and weeding. Fields were fertilized; arid lands irrigated. The agricultural arts evolved in two stages: horticulture, or garden culture with the dibble and hoe; and agriculture, or field culture with the plow. In the earlier stage, the cultivation of plants was probably the work of women. As dependence upon garden produce increased, cultivation grew in importance and in many instances passed into the hands of men. This was true particularly where the plow was used. Thus the agricultural arts were developed. Beginning in Neolithic times, they had grown in the relatively short period of a few thousand years to maturity and had produced the great urban, metallurgical, literate, calendrical civilizations of antiquity.

The observations just made concerning the origin of agriculture will apply also to the origin of animal husbandry. The domestication of animals is not to be thought of as the result of an idea which flashed across some man's mind about 10,000 B.C. It was not the result of a sudden discovery, either of fact or of concept. Man had been living in intimate association with other animal species for hundreds of thousands of years. We know from studies of preliterate cultures of the modern world that even the most primitive of peoples have a great deal of accurate and detailed knowledge of the fauna of their habitats, and it is a reasonable inference that all tribes, thousands of years before domestication began, had a comparable knowledge of the animal species in their own localities. Animal husbandry, like agriculture, is most profitably to be regarded as a change in the relationship between man and the other animal species with which he was associated. The domestication of animals is merely the imposition and extension of cultural control over the lives of certain animal species.

It has often been assumed that the domestication of animals was motivated by rational and utilitarian considerations, and there is no doubt but that they played a part, perhaps the principal role, in the process. But there are reasons for believing that this is not the whole story. Some primitive peoples keep domestic animals or fowls for use in magical rituals, and domestication may, in some instances, have grown out of such practices. Again, some primitive peoples keep various animals—birds and reptiles as well as mammals—as pets. Domestication may have been initiated in this way in some instances. And with regard to utilitarian motives, we have already noted [(White 1959b: Chap. 2)] that the ancestors of our domesticated sheep had no wool, or at least none suitable for textile purposes, and cattle were not milked until centuries after their domestication (Lowie 1940:41, 51-52)—although, of course, both sheep and cattle could have been kept for meat.

It seems best, therefore, to assume that more than one factor, or motive, played a part in the domestication of animals. Furthermore, it seems reasonable to think of not one single occurrence of domestication, but of a few or several. In some instances magical or ritual reasons may have been uppermost. In others, as Morgan long ago suggested, it may have resulted from "the capture of the young of . . . animals and rearing them, not unlikely, from the merest freak of fancy" (Morgan 1877:42). But whatever factors may have established the symbiotic relationship between man and other animals in the first place, we may be sure that it was practical and utilitarian considerations that developed, expanded, and extended these relationships later, in the art of animal husbandry. The relationship between man and other species had of course been close and intimate for a very long time. Man had depended, in varying degrees, upon animals for food and other valuable and useful materials for hundreds of thousands of years prior to domestication. The exploitation and utilization of the fauna of a region is a form of control over nature exercised by man. The domestication of animals is merely an enlargement and an intensification of this relationship of control as the consequence of the introduction of a new principle: keeping animals alive for use instead of killing them for use. This change in the relationship between man and certain other animal species was no doubt brought about by the same factors which initiated and established agriculture.

In regions where both agriculture and animal husbandry were established, the latter did much to complement the former, as well as to make a distinctive contribution of its own. Beasts could be used to draw plows or vehicles and as motive power for irrigation pumps and grinding mills. Their dung could be used for fertilizer or for fuel. Livestock could be fed in part on cultivated plants. Meat and milk provided a staple and nutritious food supply in many cultural systems. Thus, in some regions, agriculture primarily or alone, in others, agriculture and animal husbandry together, provided the motive force for the First Great Cultural Revolution.

NOTE

[1]V. Gordon Childe (1946:36, 41), Braidwood (1948:72, 76-81). The Braidwoods have suggested that agriculture may not have originated in the fertile river valleys of the Old · World as previously supposed, but on the "hilly flanks" of these regions (Braidwood and Braidwood 1949:665).

The origin of the state is a problem that has long intrigued anthropologists, historians, and other scholars. The following essay by Robert L. Carneiro discusses and rejects all previous theories on the subject and then goes on to propose an exciting new theory that explains, among other things, why states arose in some areas but not in others.

Because warfare figures prominently in Carneiro's theory, we suggest that the reader consult Keith Otterbein's recent The Evolution of War (1970). We also recommend Morton Fried's "On the Evolution of Social Stratification and the State" (1960; B-M, A-293) and The Evolution of Political Society (1967). Advanced students should also consult Adams (1955; B-M, E-1), Carneiro (1962), Kenyon (1959; B-M, A-380), Naroll (1956), Steward (1949; B-M, A-216), and Tatje and Naroll (1970).

Two: 3

A Theory of the Origin of the State

For the first 2 million years of his existence, man lived in bands or villages which, as far as we can tell, were completely autonomous. Not until perhaps 5000 B.C. did villages begin to aggregate into larger political units. But, once this process of aggregation began, it continued at a progressively faster pace and led, around 4000 B.C., to the formation of the first state in history. (When I speak of a state I mean an autonomous political unit, encompassing many communites within its territory and having a centralized government with the power to collect taxes, draft men for work or war, and decree and enforce laws.)

Although it was by all odds the most far-reaching political development in human history, the origin of the state is still very imperfectly understood. Indeed, not one of the current theories of the rise of the state is entirely satisfactory. At one point or another, all of them fail. There is one theory, though, which I believe does provide a convincing explanation of how states began. It is a theory which I proposed once before (Carneiro 1961), and which I present here more fully. Before doing so, however, it seems desirable to discuss, if only briefly, a few of the traditional theories.

Explicit theories of the origin of the state are relatively modern. Classical writers like Aristotle, unfamiliar with other forms of political organization, tended to think of the state as "natural," and therefore as not requiring an explanation. However, the age of exploration, by making Europeans aware that many peoples throughout the world lived, not in states, but in independent villages or tribes, made the state seem less natural, and thus more in need of explanation.

*Reprinted with the permission of the author and publisher from *Science*, Vol. 169, 21 August 1970, pp. 733-738. Copyright 1970 by the American Association for the Advancement of Science.

Robert L. Carneiro is Curator of South American Ethnology at the American Museum of Natural History, New York.

Of the many modern theories of state origins that have been proposed, we can consider only a few. Those with a racial basis, for example, are now so thoroughly discredited that they need not be dealt with here. We can also reject the belief that the state is an expression of the "genius" of a people,[1] or that it arose through a "historical accident." Such notions make the state appear to be something metaphysical or adventitious, and thus place it beyond scientific understanding. In my opinion, the origin of the state was neither mysterious nor fortuitous. It was not the product of "genius" or the result of chance, but the outcome of a regular and determinate cultural process. Moreover, it was not a unique event but a recurring phenomenon: states arose independently in different places and at different times. Where the appropriate conditions existed, the state emerged.

Voluntaristic Theories

Serious theories of state origins are of two general types: *voluntaristic* and *coercive*. Voluntaristic theories hold that, at some point in their history, certain peoples spontaneously, rationally, and voluntarily gave up their individual sovereignties to form a larger political unit deserving to be called a state. Of such theories the best known is the old Social Contract theory, which was associated especially with the name of Rousseau. We now know that no such compact was ever subscribed to by human groups, and the Social Contract theory is today nothing more than a historical curiosity.

The most widely accepted of modern voluntaristic theories is the one I call the "automatic" theory. According to this theory, the invention of agriculture automatically brought into being a surplus of food, enabling some individuals to divorce themselves from food production and to become potters, weavers, smiths, masons, and so on, thus creating an extensive division of labor. Out of this occupational specialization there developed a political integration which united a number of previously independent communities into a state. This argument was set forth most frequently by the late British archeologist V. Gordon Childe (1936:82-83; 1950:6.)

The principal difficulty with this theory is that agriculture does *not* automatically create a food surplus. We know this because many agricultural peoples of the world produce no such surplus. Virtually all Amazonian Indians, for example, were agricultural, but in aboriginal times they did not produce a food surplus. That it was *technically feasi-*

ble for them to produce such a surplus is shown by the fact that, under the stimulus of European settlers' desire for food, a number of tribes did raise manioc in amounts well above their own needs, for the purpose of trading.[2] Thus the technical means for generating a food surplus were there; it was the social mechanisms needed to actualize it that were lacking.

Another current voluntaristic theory of state origins is Karl Wittfogel's "hydraulic hypothesis." As I understand him, Wittfogel sees the state arising in the following way. In certain arid and semiarid areas of the world, where village farmers had to struggle to support themselves by means of small-scale irrigation, a time arrived when they saw that it would be to the advantage of all concerned to set aside their individual autonomies and merge their villages into a single large political unit capable of carrying out irrigation on a broad scale. The body of officials they created to devise and administer such extensive irrigation works brought the state into being.[3]

This theory has recently run into difficulties. Archeological evidence now makes it appear that in at least three of the areas that Wittfogel cites as exemplifying his "hydraulic hypothesis"—Mesopotamia, China, and Mexico—full-fledged states developed well before large-scale irrigation.[4] Thus, irrigation did not play the causal role in the rise of the state that Wittfogel appears to attribute to it.[5]

This and all other voluntaristic theories of the rise of the state founder on the same rock: the demonstrated inability of autonomous political units to relinquish their sovereignty in the absence of overriding external constraints. We see this inability manifested again and again by political units ranging from tiny villages to great empires. Indeed, one can scan the pages of history without finding a single genuine exception to this rule. Thus, in order to account for the origin of the state we must set aside voluntaristic theories and look elsewhere.

Coercive Theories

A close examination of history indicates that only a coercive theory can account for the rise of the state. Force, and not enlightened self-interest, is the mechanism by which political evolution has led, step by step, from autonomous villages to the state.

The view that war lies at the root of the state is by no means new. Twenty-five hundred years ago Heraclitus wrote that "war is the father of all things." The first careful study of the role of warfare in the rise of the state, however, was made less than a hundred years ago, by Herbert Spencer in his *Principles of Sociology* (see Carneiro 1967:32-47, 63-96, 153-165). Perhaps better known than Spencer's writings on war and the state are the conquest theories of continental writers such as Ludwig Gumplowicz (1893), Gustav Ratzenhofer (1893), and Franz Oppenheimer (1926).

Oppenheimer, for example, argued that the state emerged when the productive capacity of settled agriculturalists was combined with the energy of pastoral nomads through the conquest of the former by the latter (1926:51-55). This theory, however, has two serious defects. First, it fails to account for the rise of states in aboriginal America, where pastoral nomadism was unknown. Second, it is now well established that pastoral nomadism did not arise in the Old World until after the earliest states had emerged.

Regardless of deficiencies in particular coercive theories, however, there is little question that, in one way or another, war played a decisive role in the rise of the state. Historical or archeological evidence of war is found in the early stages of state formation in Mesopotamia, Egypt, India, China, Japan, Greece, Rome, northern Europe, central Africa, Polynesia, Middle America, Peru, and Colombia, to name only the most prominent examples.

Thus, with the Germanic kingdoms of northern Europe especially in mind, Edward Jenks observed that, "historically speaking, there is not the slightest difficulty in proving that all political communities of the modern type [that is, states] owe their existence to successful warfare" (1900:73). And in reading Jan Vansina's *Kingdoms of the Savanna* (1966), a book with no theoretical ax to grind, one finds that state after state in central Africa arose in the same manner.

But is it really true that there is no exception to this rule? Might there not be, somewhere in the world, an example of a state which arose without the agency of war?

Until a few years ago, anthropologists generally believed that the Classic Maya provided such an instance. The archeological evidence then available gave no hint of warfare among the early Maya and led scholars to regard them as a peace-loving theocratic state which had arisen entirely without war.[6] However, this view is no longer tenable. Recent archeological discoveries have placed the Classic Maya in a very different light. First came the discovery of the Bonampak murals, showing the early Maya at war and reveling in the torture of war captives. Then, excavations around Tikal revealed large earthworks partly surrounding that Classic Maya city, pointing clearly to a military rivalry with the neighboring city of Uaxactún (Puleston and Callender 1967:45, 47). Summarizing present thinking on the subject, Michael D. Coe has observed that "the ancient Maya were just as warlike as the . . . bloodthirsty states of the Post-Classic" (1966:147).

Yet, though warfare is surely a prime mover in the origin of the state, it cannot be the only factor. After all, wars have been fought in many parts of the world where the state never emerged. Thus, while warfare may be a necessary condition for the rise of the state, it is not a sufficient one. Or, to put it another way, while we can identify war as the *mechanism* of state formation, we need also to specify the *conditions* under which it gave rise to the state.

Environmental Circumscription

How are we to determine these conditions? One promising approach is to look for those factors common to areas of the world in which states arose indigenously—areas such as the Nile, Tigris-Euphrates, and Indus valleys in the Old World and the Valley of Mexico and the mountain and coastal valleys of Peru in the New. These areas differ from one another in many ways—in altitude, temperature, rainfall, soil type, drainage pattern, and many other features. They do, however, have one thing in common: *they are all areas of circumscribed agricultural land.* Each of them is set off by mountains, seas, or deserts, and these environmental features sharply delimit the area that simple farming peoples could occupy and cultivate. In this respect these areas are very different from, say, the Amazon basin or the eastern woodlands of North America, where extensive and unbroken forests provided almost unlimited agricultural land.

But what is the significance of circumscribed agricultural land for the origin of the state? Its significance can best be understood by comparing political development in two regions of the world having contrasting ecologies—one a region with circumscribed agricultural land and the other a region where there was extensive and unlimited land. The two areas I have chosen to use in making this comparison are the coastal valleys of Peru and the Amazon basin.

Our examination begins at the stage where agricultural communities were already present but where each was still completely autonomous. Looking first at the Amazon basin, we see that agricultural villages there were numerous, but widely dispersed. Even in areas with relatively dense clustering, like the Upper Xingú basin, villages were at least 10 or 15 miles apart. Thus, the typical Amazonian community, even though it practiced a simple form of shifting cultivation which required extensive amounts of land, still had around it all the forest land needed for its gardens (see Carneiro 1960). For Amazonia as a whole, then, population density was low and subsistence pressure on the land was slight.

Warfare was certainly frequent in Amazonia, but it was waged for reasons of revenge, the taking of women, the gaining of personal prestige, and motives of a similar sort. There being no shortage of land, there was, by and large, no warfare over land.

The consequences of the type of warfare that did occur in Amazonia were as follows. A defeated group was not, as a rule, driven from its land. Nor did the victor make any real effort to subject the vanquished, or to exact tribute from him. This would have been difficult to accomplish in any case, since there was no effective way to prevent the losers from fleeing to a distant part of the forest. Indeed, defeated villages often chose to do just this, not so much to avoid subjugation as to avoid further attack. With settlement so sparse in Amazonia, a new area of forest could be found and occupied with relative ease, and without trespassing on the territory of another village. Moreover, since virtually any area of forest is suitable for cultivation, subsistence agriculture could be carried on in the new habitat just about as well as in the old.

It was apparently by this process of fight and flight that horticultural tribes gradually spread out until they came to cover, thinly but extensively, almost the entire Amazon basin. Thus, under the conditions of unlimited agricultural land and low population density that prevailed in Amazonia, the effect of warfare was to disperse villages over a wide area, and to keep them autonomous. With only a very few exceptions, noted below, there was no tendency in Amazonia for villages to be held in place and to combine into larger political units.

In marked contrast to the situation in Amazonia were the events that transpired in the narrow valleys of the Peruvian coast. The reconstruction of these events that I present is admittedly inferential, but I think it is consistent with the archeological evidence.

Here too our account begins at the stage of small, dispersed, and autonomous farming communities. However, instead of being scattered over a vast expanse of rain forest as they were in Amazonia, villages here were confined to some 78 short and narrow valleys.[7] Each of these valleys, moreover, was backed by the mountains, fronted by the sea, and flanked on either side by desert as dry as any in the world. Nowhere else, perhaps, can one find agricultural valleys more sharply circumscribed than these.

As with neolithic communites generally, villages of the Peruvian coastal valleys tended to grow in size. Since autonomous villages are likely to fission as they grow, as long as land is available for the settlement of splinter communities, these villages undoubtedly split from time to time.[8] Thus, villages tended to increase in number faster than they grew in size. This increase in the number of villages occupying a valley probably continued, without giving rise to significant changes in subsistence practices, until all the readily arable land in the valley was being farmed.

At this point two changes in agricultural techniques began to occur: the tilling of land already under cultivation was intensified, and new, previously unusable land was brought under cultivation by means of terracing and irrigation (see Carneiro 1958).

Yet the rate at which new arable land was created failed to keep pace with the increasing demand for it. Even before the land shortage became so acute that irrigation began to be practiced systematically, villages were undoubtedly already fighting one another over land. Prior to this time, when agricultural villages were still few in number and well supplied with land, the warfare waged in the coastal valleys of Peru had probably been of much the same type as that described above for Amazonia. With increasing pressure of human population on the land, however, the major incentive for war changed from a desire for revenge to a need to acquire land. And, as the causes of war became predominantly economic, the frequency, intensity, and importance of war increased.

Once this stage was reached, a Peruvian village that lost a war faced consequences very different from those faced by a defeated village in Amazonia. There, as we have seen, the vanquished could flee to a new locale, subsisting there about as well as they had subsisted before, and retaining their independence. In Peru, however, this alternative was no longer open to the inhabitants of defeated villages. The mountains, the desert, and the sea—to say nothing of neighboring villages— blocked escape in every direction. A village defeated in war thus faced only grim prospects. If it was allowed to remain on its own land, instead of being exterminated or expelled, this concession came only at a price. And the price was political subordination to the victor. This subordination generally entailed at least the payment of a tribute or tax in kind, which the defeated village could provide only by producing more food than it had produced before. But subordination sometimes involved a further loss of autonomy on the part of the defeated village—namely, incorporation into the political unit dominated by the victor.

Through the recurrence of warfare of this type, we see arising in coastal Peru integrated territorial units transcending the village in size and in degree of organization. Political evolution was attaining the level of the chiefdom.

As land shortages continued and became even more acute, so did warfare. Now, however, the competing units were no longer small villages but, often, large chiefdoms. From this point on, through the conquest of chiefdom by chiefdom, the size of political units increased at a progressively faster rate. Naturally, as autonomous political units increased in size, they decreased in number, with the result that an entire valley was eventually unified under the banner of its strongest chiefdom. The political unit thus formed was undoubtedly sufficiently centralized and complex to warrant being called a state.

The political evolution I have described for one valley of Peru was also taking place in other valleys, in the highlands as well as on the coast.[9] Once valley-wide kingdoms emerged, the next step was the formation of miltivalley kingdoms through the conquest of weaker valleys by stronger ones. The culmination of this process was the conquest[10] of all of Peru by its most powerful state, and the formation of a single great empire. Although this step may have occurred once or twice before in Andean history, it was achieved most notably, and for the last time, by the Incas.[11]

Political Evolution

While the aggregation of villages into chiefdoms, and of chiefdoms into kingdoms, was occurring by external acquisiton, the structure of these increasingly larger political units was being elaborated by internal evolution. These inner changes were, of course, closely related to outer events. The expansion of successful states brought within their borders conquered peoples and territory which had to be administered. And it was the individuals who had distinguished themselves in war who were generally appointed to political office and assigned the task of carrying out this administration. Besides maintaining law and order and collecting taxes, the functions of this burgeoning class of administrators included mobilizing labor for building irrigation works, roads, fortresses, palaces, and temples. Thus, their functions helped to weld an assorted collection of petty states into a single integrated and centralized political unit.

These same individuals, who owed their improved social position to their exploits in war, became, along with the ruler and his kinsmen, the nucleus of an upper class. A lower class in turn emerged from the prisoners taken in war and employed as servants and slaves by their captors. In this manner did war contribute to the rise of social classes.

I noted earlier that peoples attempt to acquire their neighbors' land before they have made the fullest possible use of their own. This implies that every autonomous village has an untapped margin of food productivity, and that this margin is squeezed out only when the village is subjugated and compelled to pay taxes in kind. The surplus food extracted from conquered villages through taxation, which in the aggregate attained very significant proportions, went largely to support the ruler, his warriors and retainers, officials, priests, and other members of the rising upper class, who thus became completely divorced from food production.

Finally, those made landless by war but not enslaved tended to gravitate to settlements which, because of their specialized administrative, commercial or religious functions, were growing into towns and cities. Here they were able to make a living as workers and artisans, exchanging their labor or their wares for part of the economic surplus extracted from village farmers by the ruling class and spent by members of that class to raise their standard of living.

The process of political evolution which I have outlined for the coastal valleys of Peru was, in its essential features, by no means unique to this region. Areas of circumscribed agricultural land elsewhere in the world, such as the Valley of Mexico, Mesopotamia, the Nile Valley, and the Indus Valley, saw the process occur in much the same way and for essentially the same reasons. In these areas, too, autonomous neolithic villages were succeeded by chiefdoms, chiefdoms by kingdoms, and kingdoms by empires. The last stage of this development was, of course, the most impressive. The scale and magnificence attained by the early empires overshadowed everything that had gone before. But, in a sense, empires were merely the logical culmination of the process. The really fundamental step, the one that had triggered the entire train of events that led to empires, was the change from village autonomy to supravillage integration. This step was a change in kind; everything that followed was, in a way, only a change in degree.

In addition to being pivotal, the step to supracommunity aggregation was difficult, for it took 2 million years to achieve. But, once it was achieved, once village autonomy was transcended, only two or three millennia were required for the rise of great empires and the flourishing of complex civilizations.

Resource Concentration

Theories are first formulated on the basis of a limited number of facts. Eventually, though, a theory must confront all of the facts. And often new facts are stubborn and do not conform to the theory, or do not conform very well. What distinguishes a successful theory from an unsuccessful one is that it can be modified or elaborated to accomodate the entire range of facts. Let us see how well the "circumscription theory" holds up when it is brought face-to-face with certain facts that appear to be exceptions.

For the first test let us return to Amazonia. Early voyagers down the Amazon left written testimony of a culture along that river higher than the culture I have described for Amazonia generally. In the 1500's, the native population living on the banks of the Amazon was relatively dense, villages were fairly large and close together, and some degree of social stratification existed. Moreover, here and there a paramount chief held sway over many communities.

The question immediately arises: With unbroken stretches of arable land extending back from the Amazon for hundreds of miles, why were there chiefdoms here?

To answer this question we must look closely at the environmental conditions afforded by the Amazon. Along the margins of the river itself, and on islands within it, there is a type of land called *várzea*. The river floods this land every year, covering it with a layer of fertile silt. Because of this annual replenishment, *várzea* is agricultural land of first quality which can be cultivated year after year without ever having to lie fallow. Thus, among native farmers it was highly prized and greatly coveted. The waters of the Amazon were also extraordinarily bountiful, providing fish, manatees, turtles and turtle eggs, caimans, and other riverine foods in inexhaustible amounts. By virtue of this concentration of resources, the Amazon, as a habitat, was distinctly superior to its hinterlands.

Concentration of resources along the Amazon amounted almost to a kind of circumscription. While there was no sharp cleavage between productive and unproductive land, as there was in Peru, there was at least a steep ecological gradient. So much more rewarding was the Amazon River than adjacent areas, and so desirable did it become as a habitat, that peoples were drawn to it from surrounding regions. Eventually crowding occurred along many portions of the river, leading to warfare over sections of river front. And the losers in war, in order to retain access to the river, often had no choice but to submit to the victors. By this subordination of villages to a paramount chief there arose along the Amazon chiefdoms representing a higher step in political evolution than had occurred elsewhere in the basin.[12]

The notion of resource concentration also helps to explain the surprising degree of political development apparently attained by peoples of the Peruvian coast while they were still depending primarily on fishing for subsistence, and only secondarily on agriculture. Of this seeming anomaly Lanning has written: "To the best of my knowledge, this is the only case in which so many of the characteristics of civilization have been found without a basically agricultural economic foundation" (1967:59).

Armed with the concept of resource concentration, however, we can show that this development was not so anomalous after all. The explanation, it seems to me, runs as follows. Along the coast of Peru wild food sources occurred in considerable number and variety. However, they were restricted to a very narrow margin of land.[13] Accordingly, while the *abundance* of food in this zone led to a sharp rise in population, the *restrictedness* of this food soon resulted in the almost complete occupation of exploitable areas. And when pressure on the available resources reached a critical level, competitition over land ensued. The result of this competition was to set in motion the sequence of events of political evolution that I have described.

Thus, it seems that we can safely add resource concentration to environmental circumscription as a factor leading to warfare over land, and thus to political integration beyond the village level.

Social Circumscription

But there is still another factor to be considered in accounting for the rise of the state.

In dealing with the theory of environmental circumscription while discussing the Yanomamö Indians of Venezuela, Napoleon A. Chagnon (1968:249, 251; see also Fock 1964:52) has introduced the concept of "social circumscription." By this he means that a high density of population in an area can produce effects on peoples living near the center of the area that are similar to effects produced by environomental circumscription. This notion seems to me to be an important addition to our theory. Let us see how, according to Chagnon, social circumscription has operated among the Yanomamö.

The Yanomamö, who number some 10,000, live in an extensive region of noncircumscribed rain forest, away from any large river. One might expect that Yanomamö villages would thus be more or less evenly spaced. However, Chagnon notes that, at the center of Yanomamö territory, villages are closer together than they are at the periphery. Because of this, they tend to impinge on one another more, with the result that warfare is more frequent and intense in the center than in peripheral areas. Moreover, it is more difficult for villages in the nuclear area to escape attack by moving away, since, unlike villages on the periphery, their ability to move is somewhat restricted.

The net result is that villages in the central area of Yanomamö territory are larger than villages in the other areas, since large village size is an advantage for both attack and defense. A further effect of more intense warfare in the nuclear area is that village headmen are stronger in that area. Yanomamö headmen are also the war leaders, and their influence increases in proportion to their village's participation in war. In addition, offensive and defensive alliances between villages are more common in the center of Yanomamö territory than in outlying areas. Thus, while still at the autonomous village level of political organization, those Yanomamö subject to social circumscription have clearly moved a step or two in the direction of higher political development.

Although the Yanomamö manifest social circumscription only to a modest degree, this amount of it has been enough to make a difference in their level of political organization. What the effects of social circumscription would be in areas where it was more fully expressed should, therefore, be clear. First would come a reduction in the size of the territory of each village. Then, as population pressure became more severe, warfare over land would ensue. But because adjacent land for miles around was already the property of other villages, a defeated village would have nowhere to flee. From this point on, the consequences of warfare for that village, and for political evolution in general, would be essentially as I have described them for the situation of environmental circumscription.

To return to Amazonia, it is clear that, if social circumscription is operative among the Yanomamö today, it was certainly operative among the tribes of the Amazon River 400 years ago. And its effect would undoubtedly have been to give a further spur to political evolution in that region.

We see then that, even in the absence of sharp environmental circumscription, the factors of resource concentration and social circumscription may, by intensifying war and redirecting it toward the taking of land, give a strong impetus to political development.

With these auxiliary hypotheses incorporated into it, the circumscription theory is now better able to confront the entire range of test cases that can be brought before it. For example, it can now account for the rise of the state in the Hwang Valley of northern China, and even in the Petén region of the Maya lowlands, areas not characterized by strictly circumscribed agricultural land. In the case of the Hwang Valley, there is no question that resource concentration and social circumscription were present and active forces. In the lowland Maya area, resource concentration seems not to have been a major factor, but social circumscription may well have been.

Some archeologists may object that population density in the Petén during Formative times was too low to give rise to social circumscription. But, in assessing what constitutes a population dense enough to produce this effect, we must consider not so much the total land area occupied as the amount of land needed to support the existing population. And the size of this supporting area depends not only on the size of the population but also on the mode of subsistence. The shifting cultivation presumably practiced by the ancient Maya (Morely and Brainerd 1956:128-129) required considerably more land, per capita, than did the permanent field cultivation of say, the Valley of Mexico or the coast of Peru.[14] Consequently, insofar as its effects are concerned, a relatively low population density in the Petén may have been equivalent to a much higher one in Mexico or Peru.

We have already learned from the Yanomamö example that social circumscription may begin to operate while population is still relatively sparse. And we can be sure that the Petén was far more densely peopled in Formative times than Yanomamö territory is today. Thus, population density among the lowland Maya, while giving a superficial appearance of sparseness, may actually have been high enough to provoke fighting over land, and thus provide the initial impetus for the formation of a state.

Conclusion

In summary, then, the circumscription theory in its elaborated form goes far toward accounting for the origin of the state. It explains why states arose where they did, and why they failed to arise elsewhere. It shows the state to be a predictable response to certain specific cultural, demographic, and ecological conditions. Thus, it helps to elucidate what was undoubtedly the most important single step ever taken in the political evolution of mankind.

NOTES

[1] For example, the early American sociologist Lester F. Ward saw the state as "the result of an extraordinary exercise of the rational . . . faculty" which seemed to him so exceptional that "it must have been the emanation of a single brain or a few concerting minds. . . ." (1883:Vol. 2:224).

[2] I have in my files recorded instances of surplus food production by such Amazonian tribes as the Tupinambá, Jevero, Mundurucú, Tucano, Desana, Cubeo, and Canela. An exhuastive search of the ethnographic literature for this region would undoubtedly reveal many more examples.

[3] Wittfogel states: "These patterns [of organization and social control—that is, the state] come into being when an experimenting community of farmers or protofarmers finds large sources of moisture in a dry but potentially fertile area . . . a number of farmers eager to conquer [agriculturally, not militarily] arid lowlands and plains are forced to invoke the organizational devices which—on the basis of premachine technology—offer the one chance of success; they must work in cooperation with their fellows and subordinate themselves to a directing authority" (1957:18).

[4] For Mesopotamia, Robert M. Adams has concluded: "In short, there is nothing to suggest that the rise of dynastic authority in southern Mesopotamia was linked to the administrative requirements of a major canal system" (Adams 1960:281). For China, the prototypical area for Wittfogel's hydraulic theories, the French Sinologist Jacques Gernet has recently written: "although the establishment of a system of regulation of water courses and irrigation, and the control of this system, may have affected the political constitution of the military states and imperial China, the fact remains that, historically, it was the pre-existing state structures and the large, well-trained labour force provided by the armies that made the great irrigation projects possible" (1968:92). For Mexico, large-scale irrigation systems do not appear to antedate the Classic period, whereas it is clear that the first states arose in the preceding Formative or Pre-Classic period.

[5] This is not to say, of course, that large-scale irrigation, where it occurred, did not contribute significantly to increasing the power and scope of the state. It unquestionably did. To the extent that Wittfogel limits himself to this contention, I have no quarrel with him whatever. However, the point at issue is not how the state increased its power but how it arose in the first place. And to this issue the hydraulic hypothesis does not appear to hold the key.

[6] For example, Julian H. Steward wrote: "It is possible, therefore, that the Maya were able to develop a high civilization only because they enjoyed an unusually long period of peace; for their settlement pattern would seem to have been too vulnerable to warfare" (1949:17).

[7] In early agricultural times (Preceramic Period VI, beginning about 2500 B.C.) human

settlement seems to have been denser along the coast than in the river valleys, and subsistence appears to have been based more on fishing than on farming. Furthermore, some significant first steps in political evolution beyond autonomous villages may have been taken at this stage. However, once subsistence began to be based predominantly on agriculture, the settlement pattern changed, and communities were thenceforth concentrated more in the river valleys, where the only land of any size suitable for cultivation was located (see Lanning 1967:57-59).

[8]In my files I find reported instances of village splitting among the following Amazonian tribes: Kuikuru, Amarakaeri, Cubeo, Urubú, Tuparí, Yanomamõ, Tucano, Tenetehara, Canela, and Northern Cayapó. Under the conditions of easy resettlement found in Amazonia, splitting often takes place at a village population level of less than 100, and village size seldom exceeds 200. In coastal Peru, however, where land was severely restricted, villages could not fission so readily, and thus grew to population levels which, according to Lanning (1967:64), may have averaged over 300.

[9]Naturally, this evolution took place in the various Peruvian valleys at different rates and to different degrees. In fact it is possible that at the same time that some valleys were already unified politically, others still had not evolved beyond the stage of autonomous villages.

[10]Not every step in empire building was necessarily taken through actual physical conquest, however. The threat of force sometimes had the same effect as its exercise. In this way many smaller chiefdoms and states were probably coerced into giving up their sovereignty without having to be defeated on the field of battle. Indeed, it was an explicit policy of the Incas, in expanding their empire, to try persuasion before resorting to force of arms (see Garcilaso de la Vega 1966:108, 111, 140, 143, 146, 264).

[11]The evolution of empire in Peru was thus by no means rectilinear or irreversible. Advance alternated with decline. Integration was sometimes followed by disintegration, with states fragmenting back to autonomous villages. But the forces underlying political development were strong and, in the end, prevailed. Thus, despite fluctuations and reversions, the course of evolution in Peru was unmistakable: it began with many small, simple, scattered, and autonomous communities and ended with a single, vast, complex, and centralized empire.

[12]Actually, a similar political development did take place in another part of Amazonia—the basin of the Mamoré River in the Mojos plain of Bolivia. Here, too, resource concentration appears to have played a key role (see Denevan 1966:43-50, 104-105, 108-110). In native North America north of Mexico the highest cultural development attained, Middle-Mississippi, also occurred along a major river (the Mississippi), which, by providing especially fertile soil and riverine food resources, comprised a zone of resource concentration (see Griffin 1967:189).

[13]Resource concentration, then, was here combined with environmental circumscription. And, indeed, the same thing can be said of the great desert river valleys, such as the Nile, Tigris-Euphrates, and Indus.

[14]One can assume, I think, that any substantial increase in population density among the Maya was accompanied by a certain intensification of agriculture. As the population increased fields were probably weeded more thoroughly, and they may well have been cultivated a year or two longer and fallowed a few years less. Yet, given the nature of soils in the humid tropics, the absence of any evidence of fertilization, and the moderate population densities, it seems likely that Maya farming remained extensive rather than becoming intensive.

Anthropologists have long regarded surplus as a prime-mover of cultural evolution. Recently, Robert Carneiro (1970; and this volume) and Michael Harner (1970) have argued in favor of scarcity as a major force. Both also argue for the importance of competition in one form or another. Like Service's essay, which heads this section on prime-movers, the following essay by Isaac raises the question of whether any invariant relationship exists between such factors as scarcity, surplus, cooperation, and competition in the course of sociocultural evolution.

Meggers' (1954) well-known exposition of the surplus argument is available in the Bobbs-Merrill Reprint Series (B-M, S-189), as is Ferdon's (1959) cogent criticism of her essay (B-M, A-64). Students who wish to pursue the surplus controversy further should consult Pearson (1957), Dalton (1960; B-M, A-107), Harris (1959; B-M, A-107—bound with Dalton's essay), and Orans (1966). Langer's (1972) article on population pressure and infanticide in Europe during the period 1750-1850 provides stimulating material for lecture or classroom discussion. Advanced students should read with care Harner's essay (1970).

Two:4

Resource Scarcity, Competition, and Cooperation in Cultural Evolution

Barry L. Isaac*

I

It has long been a truism in anthropology that one of the basic mechanisms—if not, indeed, *the* mechanism—of sociocultural evolution was the production of economic surplus, largely made possible by the "Neolithic (Agricultural) Revolution."[1] This surplus production enabled some people to become non-producers and to specialize in the areas of politics, warfare, religion, crafts, and fine arts, among other things. Political, religious, and military specialists, through the adroit and self-seeking use of this surplus production, eventually subjugated producer populations and welded them into states or great empires.[2]

Although this theory is commonly associated with the British prehistorian V. Gordon Childe (1936, 1946), most modern anthropologists appear to have some commitment to it. In recent years the surplus theory has been represented most prominently by American archeologist Betty Meggers' work on environmental potential and cultural development. Meggers has argued that the "cradles of civilization" all belonged to "areas of unlimited agricultural potential" (her "Type 4 Areas") which allowed for the development of extractive methods that ". . . were so productive that many thousands of commoners could be levied for military service, labor on public works or similar specialized tasks that contributed nothing to the basic subsistence" (Meggers 1954:811).

Perhaps the best indicator of the firm entrenchment of the surplus theory in anthropology is the fact that Edwin Ferdon's (1959) brilliant

*Written especially for this volume.

Barry L. Isaac is assistant professor of anthropology at the University of Cincinnati.

We regret that the excellent symposium on evolution published in *Social Biology* in 1972 did not come to our attention until too late to include discussion of it here.

refutation of Meggers' argument has received much less notice. Ferdon showed that "there is very little, if any, correlation between potential ratings and cultural achievement. . . . If anything is brought out . . . it is that high cultural development has come about in areas considerably less than perfect for agriculture under natural conditions" (Ferdon 1959:12). Even though Ferdon's article was published in a prominent journal in the field (*Southwestern Journal of Anthropology*) and has since been made readily available in the Bobbs-Merrill Reprint Series (as has Meggers' article), it seems to be relatively rarely cited; whereas Meggers' argument is cited again and again in the literature.

To my knowledge, the surplus theory was not thoroughly and critically examined until the debate among Pearson (1957), Harris (1959), and Dalton (1960), which in some ways ended in a standoff.[3] True, some clarification of terminology emerged (see, especially, Dalton 1960), and a cautionary note was sounded: "No simple relationship is foreseen . . . between the size of the surplus above subsistence and the appearance of stratified and specialized phenomena" (Harris 1959:196). On the whole, however, "the basic assumption of the surplus theory remains unchanged—namely, that variations in productivity provide the most promising line of investigation for establishing cross-cultural regularities, sociocultural typologies, and both multilinear and universal evolutionary sequences" (Harris 1959:195).

Two recent articles, by Michael Harner (1970) and Robert Carneiro (1970; and this volume), have shed considerable new light on the topic. Because Carneiro's article is included in this volume, I shall not reiterate his argument here. Harner's article is difficult to summarize, and I hope my distilling it to a few paragraphs does not do it too much injustice.

Harner proposes ". . . that an inverse correlation exists between the degree of dependence on hunting and gathering and the degree of population pressure in societies having any agriculture, and that the total degree of dependence on hunting and gathering in such societies provides a scale for measuring population pressure" (1970:71). Applying this index to three samples from the "Ethnographic Atlas," he shows that as population pressure on resources increases: (1) so does the level of political integration; (2) so does the extent of class stratification; and, less important to our purpose here, (3) there is an increasing tendency toward unilineal, as opposed to cognatic, descent systems. These developments occur because:

Continuing growth of population pressure will lead to greater land subsistence resource scarcity, with consequently intensified competition for its control. In its intra-group form, such com- petitition will lead to unequal individual success in obtaining ownership or control of subsistence-producing land. At first, this may simply take the form of managerial functions within a descent group. . . . As competition grows further, class strati- fication and political integration will develop into increasingly complex forms. . . . Growth of class stratification, which can be viewed primarily (although not exclusively) as based on intra- societal competition, will thus be accompanied by the evolution of larger political units deriving (although, again, not exclusive- ly) from the increasing development of intersocietal competition as well (Harner 1970:69).

Harner feels that he has succeeded in formulating:

. . . a single general theoretical framework which has been suc- cessful in predicting evolution in descent as well as in political organization and class stratification. In this it contrasts with existing theories based upon concepts of surplus or simple en- ergy growth, which have consistently failed to explain, in terms of a single process, evolution in these three aspects of social structure. It is suggested that the natural resouce scarcity model is a representation of a process which has been extremely power- ful in human history, and that it provides an excellent basis for understanding and predicting social evolution (Harner 1970: 84-85).

In summary, Harner's argument is much like Carneiro's. Both stress resource scarcity, relative to population size, and competition as mech- hanisms of sociocultural evolution. Both have dispensed with the sur- plus theory, as well as with theories that would stress "voluntaristic" intersocietal arrangements, as explanations of social evolution—at least as regards agriculturalists. They do so with considerable force, leaving little doubt that scarcity and conflict have figured prominently in the evolution of society.

Nevertheless, I feel a certain unease about accepting their arguments too literally. Are we now to assume that surplus has played no role in sociocultural evolution? Are we now to assume that inter-group cooperation (or alliance, if one prefers) has not been important in man's sociocultural development? I think that before we arrive at any such drastic conclusions, we should return briefly to that favorite laboratory of social anthropology—the primitive, relatively simple, non-agricultural peoples—with an eye toward focusing additional light on the evolutionary process, and particularly, on how it is set in motion. I agree with Lee and DeVore (1968:12) that the study of such peoples may help us to understand better how such complex institutions as property, government, and the state came into being.

For this purpose I shall discuss the Bushmen of the Dobe area of Botswana and the much more complex, but still pre-Neolithic, Coast Salish and Southern Kwakiutl of the Northwest Coast of North America. I have chosen these two groups of people because they are well-described in the literature and because they afford some sharp contrasts. The fact that neither practices agriculture makes them additionally suitable for my purpose: examining preagriculturalists may shed light on the very *beginnings* of the evolutionary process and also help put into new perspective the contribution that agriculture eventually was to make to sociocultural evolution. My aim is not to make any sweeping generalizations on the basis of these ethnographic comparisons; rather, it is the more modest one of attempting to provide some fresh insights into the evolutionary process.

II

The !Kung Bushmen of the Dobe area of Botswana live in "camps" (bands) that range in size from roughly 20 to 40 people (Lee 1968:38). Each camp is associated with one of the permanent waterholes in the region; the foraging area around the waterhole during most of the year is about 6 miles in radius. Each camp is a self-sufficient consumption unit, receiving very little foodstuffs from other camps by way of trade. On the other hand, people move freely from camp to camp. "The net effect is of a population constantly in motion. On the average, an individual spends a third of his time living only with close relatives, a third visiting other camps, and a third entertaining visitors from other camps" (Lee 1968:31).

Exploitable food resources are distributed fairly evenly over Bushman territory, that is, there is no noticeable tendency for food resources to cluster in a few places separated by wide, sterile or low-productive areas. Plant foods, which provide 60-80% of the annual diet by weight

(Lee 1968:40), are relatively abundant during most of the year within the immediate (6-mile radius) area of the waterholes—so abundant, in fact, that although tens of thousands of pounds of Mongongo nuts, which comprise 50% of the vegetable diet by weight, are gathered and eaten each year, ". . . thousands more rot on the ground each year for want of picking" (Lee 1968:33). Given the relatively even spread of resources and the ease of exploitation, food getting is not a cooperative activity. Consumption, however, is clearly a cooperative activity. Families pool their day's production, and a pattern of generalized reciprocity distributes food rather equitably over an entire camp. Surplus, in the sense of foodstuffs stored for future consumption, is minimal; ". . . food is almost always consumed within the boundaries of the local group and within forty-eight hours of its collection" (Lee 1969: 50).

Rather than the availability of food, it is water which is ". . . by far the most important ecological determinant of Bushman subsistence. The availability of plant foods is of secondary importance and the numbers and distributions of game animals are only of minor importance" (Lee 1969:56). "During the dry season (May-October) the entire population is clustered around these wells. . . . The number of camps at each well and the size of each camp changed frequently during the course of the year" (Lee 1968:31). The mean standing population per waterhole was 41, with a range from 16 to 94 (1 to 5 camps), during the dry season of 1964 when Lee took census (1969:57-58). Two of the eight waterholes in the Dobe area had no camps around them during that season. "These differences in standing population may reflect differences in the density of foodstuffs" (Lee 1969:57). Even allowing for these local variations, "The important point is that food is a constant, but distance required to reach food is a variable; it is short in the summer, fall, and early winter, and reaches its maximum in the spring" (Lee 1968:33).

The !Kung enjoy a relatively secure existence. The work week varies from 1.2 to 3.2 work days per adult, and not everyone engages in productive activities; in fact, ". . . 65 percent of the people worked 36 percent of the time, and 35 percent of the people did not work at all" during a 4-week period in which Lee kept a work diary (Lee 1969:67-68). Even with this low work load, Bushman output is 2,140 calories and 93.1 grams of protein per person per day, which exceeds by a substantial margin the Recommended Daily Allowances of 1,975 calories and 60 grams of protein per day for persons of small size and stature but vigorous activity regime (Lee 1968:39). Life is neither "nasty" nor "brutish" for the !Kung, nor is it short: "Eight percent of the population in camps (21 of 248) was determined to be over sixty years of age . . . . every camp had at least several members over forty-five years of age, and ten of the fourteen camps had members over sixty years old; the oldest person was estimated to be 82+3 years" (Lee 1969:54). Lee's evidence for the security of Bushman life ". . . assumes an added significance because this security of life was observed during the third year of one of the most severe droughts in South Africa's history" (Lee 1968: 39).[4]

The present Bushman population is clearly far below the carrying capacity of the land they inhabit. But what would happen if their population were to increase? I think there could be a considerable population increase with no effect other than an increased work load, resulting primarily from an increase in the radius of exploitation, or a decreased diet selectivity, or both (see Lee 1968:35). Of course, if the population continued to increase, a saturation point would be reached, beyond which population could no longer expand given the technological and social apparatus with which the Bushmen presently exploit their environment. What would happen then? Would warfare and resource-area conquest result? I seriously doubt that the type of resource-area conquest that Harner and, especially, Carneiro, have in mind would result here, even with great population pressure on available resources. Conquest warfare requires a relatively highly-organized fighting force of some permanence in order to administer as well as to conquer territory. Given widely scattered resources, this sort of massing is improbable.

Surely it is not merely fortuitous that Bushman camps are highly fluid in their membership. Their fluidity tends to equalize the utilization of scattered resources and to allow the population to adjust to the minor fluctuations that occur from time to time in various parts of the territory (see Lee and Devore 1968:12). The immediate effect of population pressure on resources most probably would be increased fluidity of group membership, rather than stabilization of the type necessary for territorial conquest.

Even this modification of social organization would prove ineffective beyond a certain point, however, because "a given apparatus of energy capture in relation to a specific environment has a maximum upper limit of efficiency which cannot be transcended by merely reorganizing the labor force" (Harris 1959:193). Beyond that point, the population would cease to expand—unless a new, more productive extractive technique were developed.[5] Furthermore, if population were to increase to the carrying capacity of the land during a favorable climatic cycle, severe and disruptive decimation would be likely when a period of adverse climatic conditions occurred. And these adverse climatic conditions would not need to strike the entire Bushman area to have disastrous demographic consequences if the area as a whole had attained the maximum population that could be carried on a hunting and gathering basis with a high degree of fluidity. Relying on the principles of reciprocity that make fluidity possible, those bands in the initial disaster area would overload the climatically unaffected territory of their neighbors, who in turn would overload that of the neighbors behind them, and so on. In this manner, even localized severe adversity would send ripples of disaster throughout Bushman territory. The effects would be immediate—probably too sudden to allow for the development of a new extractive technique that might compensate for the overload.

Whether or not a pattern of population increase during favorable times, followed by decline in harsh times, has actually occurred in Bushman history, we of course do not know. What we do know is that certain features of Bushman culture would seem to make it unlikely in the future. First, there is the practice of infanticide which, although of low incidence (Lee 1969:55), is still of some demographic importance; perhaps its incidence would rise if other conditions produced a tendency for population increase.[6] Second, and more important, is the very strong restraint on breeding imposed by Bushman culture. The preferred marriage pattern would certainly seem to result in low fecundity. Bushman girls are often betrothed before they are weaned and married at age eight or nine to men in their teens. The young husband lives with his wife's family, hunting for them and "raising" his bride; but he does not gain immediate sexual access to his wife.

> This system may be good for women, but it is hard on young men, who often must endure desire for years and years, waiting all through their teens and early twenties before they can possess their wives. One young man along the Kung Bushmen had been thirty when his wife had died, and he found no one else to marry except an infant girl. When we knew him he had been waiting five years for his wife to grow up, and at that time she was only about seven . . . and when he thought that he would have to wait at least four years more for her, he would get into such a

passion of desire that he would have to send his wife away for a time, lest he forget himself and break *one of the most stringent rules* (Thomas 1965:88-89; italics added).

In addition, the Bushmen provide a notable exception to the rule that sexual drives are ". . . easily satisfied in primitive society without marriage" (Service 1966:35). Bushman culture permits very little sexual gratification outside of marriage. There are no prostitutes and very few promiscuous women. Young men ". . . just have to get used to being tempted constantly but never gratified" (Thomas 1965:89).

Whether or not these restraints on breeding evolved as a response to an experienced inability of a large population to maintain itself in this area, we do not know. But it would be difficult to accept that these patterns developed as a result of whim or accident. I think it not farfetched to speculate that in the distant past the Bushmen experienced, perhaps many times, a rise of population during climatically favorable times, followed by a disastrous decimation during climatically unfavorable times; and that restraints on fecundity eventually developed as a measure to prevent the recurrence of this disastrous cycle by maintaing the population below the carrying capacity of the land by a comfortable margin.[7]

III

The Northwest Coast Culture Area (the coastal and westward drainage areas of Oregon, Washington, and British Columbia) is also an area of abundance, at least on the surface of things. This non-agricultural area has long fascinated anthropologists, not only because of its famous "potlatch," but also because it displays several features —permanent villages of more than a thousand people, marked social stratification, high degree of specialization of labor, a great art style, and so on—that usually occur only among peoples with agriculture or animal husbandry. According to the surplus argument, the reason why these features occur almost exclusively among agriculturalists is that ordinarily only settled agriculture generates the sort of surplus that allows for this type of cultural flowering. Pursuing that argument further, the Northwest Coast was not *really* an exception, because fishing was so lucrative there as to generate the same sort of surplus economy that agriculture generated elsewhere.

A closer look at the Northwest Coast reveals that ". . . while the habitat was undeniably rich, abundance did not exist the year around but only here and there and now and then. . . ." (Suttles 1968:58). In describing the Coast Salish in particular, Suttles (1960) points to four significant features that characterize the environmental setting of native culture: (1) variety of food types; (2) local variation in the occurrence of these types; (3) seasonal variation; and, (4) fluctuation from year to year, which was due in part to the regular cycles of the fish populations and in part to less predictable weather cycles. These features resulted in pronounced differences in resources among communities and put a premium on intercommunity cooperation.

> . . . the availability of food was clearly not always predictable; there were temporary unforeseen shortages and surpluses. Under all of these conditions any mechanism by which members of one community could "bank" a temporary surplus of some particular item of diet with members of another community would be advantageous. The exchange between affinals was such a mechanism (Suttles 1960:302).

A community with a temporary surplus of perishable foodstuffs had three choices, other than allowing the surplus to spoil: (1) share it among themselves (which was not always practical, when virtually everyone in the village had a surplus of the same thing (see Vayda 1961a:620)); (2) preserve it (if it was preservable, and if there was time to do so before the next harvest was due); or, (3) take it to their respective in-laws in other villages where this foodstuff was scarce and receive in return wealth items in the form of blankets, canoes, and hide shirts, among other things (Suttles 1968:66-67; see also Suttles 1960). This was the major means of converting a surplus of foodstuffs into wealth.

> Since wealth is indirectly or directly obtainable through food, then inequalities in food production will be translated into inequalities in wealth. If one community over a period of several years were to produce more food than its neighbors, it might come to have a greater part of the society's wealth. Under such circumstances the less productive communities might be unable to give wealth back in exchange for further gifts of food from the more productive one (Suttles 1960:303).

To prevent this from happening, a potlatch was given by those who had amassed large amounts of wealth. Just as surplus food was converted into wealth, surplus wealth could be converted into high status by giving it away. "And this, though the participants need not be conscious of it, by 'restoring the purchasing power' of the other communities, enables the whole process to continue" (Suttles 1960:303; cf. the general arguments to the contrary presented by Drucker and Heizer 1967).

Piddocke (1965) makes a related case for the pro-survival or subsistence function of the aboriginal potlatch among the Southern Kwakiutl, and Vayda (1967) does likewise for the "trade feasts" of the Pomo Indians of California. In the latter case, when community A had a temporary surplus of fish, acorns, or occasionally seeds, they would invite community B, which had a temporary scarcity of the particular foodstuff, to a feast at which the people of community A exchanged their surplus food for strings of beads brought by the people of community B. At some later time, community B would reciprocate when the situations of scarcity and surplus were reversed. By this means, a community could "bank" a temporary surplus of foodstuffs with the members of other communities (Vayda 1967:498).

Of course, there would be an upper limit to the size of population that even this elaborate social organization and technology could sustain. Assuming that the Northwest Coast population was below the carrying capacity of these food-banking procedures, we may ask what might have happened if the population had increased markedly. Would there have been warfare and territorial conquest? Resources would seem to have been sufficiently clustered to allow for the development and maintenance of an armed force, as well as administrative apparatus, for the purpose of conquering territory. And it would seem that the productive area was circumscribed (in Carneiro's sense), inasmuch as there was just so much stream frontage available for harvesting fish. It is not entirely impossible that at some time in the past there was warfare of an economic nature in this area, but that a peaceable alternative had evolved. It is further possible that the Northwest Coast groups in question experienced occasional rises in population during times of surplus, followed by decimations in times of scarcity, until a mechanism evolved for banking long-term, as well as temporary, surplus among neighboring communities. A feature not to be overlooked here is that resources were sufficiently clustered to allow for the maintenance of intercommunity ties through their more or less protracted and frequent renewal during a large part of the year; people could congregate and remain for a while in one spot for this purpose. This feature is notably lacking in the Bushman case, and for that matter, in the case of many hunting-gathering groups; whereas several such groups may congregate occasionally or seasonally, they cannot remain massed for long periods of time because they exhaust the immediate resources of the meeting area and are forced to disperse into smaller units (see Lee and DeVore 1968:12).

A remaining question is: Could the problem of resource variability be solved in this case by group nomadism or the type of personnel fluidity that characterizes such groups as the Bushmen? While this is a possibility, there would appear to be a major factor militating against this solution, namely, that clustering of resources tends to lead to the development of strong attachments to particular areas (see Lee and DeVore 1968:12). This would seriously reduce the possibilities of group mobility over a wide territory and, by implication, also reduce individual mobility. A pattern of highly-formalized visiting might well be the only form of mobility that could occur under these conditions.

IV

In the remainder of this essay, I shall first offer some very tentative suggestions regarding the possible evolutionary implications of surplus and scarcity. I shall then make some equally tentative suggestions concerning the nature of future enquiry into the subject.

(1) The Bushman case points up that mere surplus, considered alone, does not necessarily lead to any development of evolutionary consequence. I think this point would probably hold true for agriculturalists as well as for hunters-gatherers.

(2) By inference, the Bushman case also raises the possibility that mere scarcity, considered alone, does not necessarily lead to any development of evolutionary consequence (except, perhaps, devolution under certain conditions). Again, I think this point would probably hold true for agriculturalists and hunters-gatherers alike.

(3) The evolutionary significance of either scarcity or surplus would appear to be relative to the manner in which resources are distributed over the exploited area. A relatively even resource distribution would seem to have far different evolutionary implications than would a relatively tightly-clustered distribution of resources. I think the contrast between the Bushman situation and that of the Northwest Coast is especially useful here (cf. Carneiro, this volume).

(4) Related to the above, I would suggest that the evolutionarily important factor is not the existence of *either* surplus *or* scarcity in a given instance, but rather their joint occurrence in a relatively small

area, in which a population enjoying surplus is relatively easily accessible to a population suffering scarcity in a different micro-niche. It should be remembered that the importance of a surplus is always relative to the possibilities of its being distributed. The effects of even a large surplus are likely to be minimal if it cannot be carried to areas of scarcity, or if people suffering scarcity cannot readily come to the areas of surplus to take advantage of it. In addition to mere ease of access in terms of distance, there must also be appropriate cultural mechanisms that allow for distribution of surplus. Again, the relative degree of clustering or lack of clustering of resources characteristic of the exploited area may largely determine the type of strategy that will evolve.

(5) Sizeable surpluses apparently will not be produced, stored or distributed in the absence of strong incentives to do so. As Carneiro (this volume) has pointed out, even the advent of agriculture does not automatically create a food surplus; incentives for its production are necessary. In Carneiro's model of the origin of the state, this incentive is provided by coercive measures on the part of a conquering power.[8] In the case of certain parts of the Northwest Coast, the incentive is provided (or appears to have been provided at least initially) by long experience in a fickle environment. In contrast, the Bushmen, who live in a bountiful environment, rarely accumulate more food than can be consumed within forty-eight hours by the local camp itself.

(6) A situation of scarcity may generate either competition or cooperation—or, more likely, both. For example, potlatching on the Northwest Coast was certainly not lacking in local competitive spirit, even though it appears to have been a mechanism for the cooperative exploitation of the area as a whole. Cooperation and competition in the face of scarcity may take on a variety of other forms, among them a temporary, or even enduring, alliance of otherwise autonomous communities under a common war leader for the purpose of competing cooperatively against other groups (cf. Harner 1970:69). To cite a hypothetical example from Webb's (1968:4) exemplification of an early version of Carneiro's "Hypothesis of Limited Land Resources and the Origins of the State:"

> The warchief, who could have the right to divide spoils, would be able to take [the wealth] of defeated groups, who would be absolutely tied down by the environment. This wealth in turn would enable him to reward the followers needed to overthrow kin ties and convert tribal gifts into taxes—in a word, to subvert the tribal constitution and establish the state. Moreover, this

could all happen in gradual stages, with each new acquisition of power representing only a small departure from current practice, so that by the time that the remnants of the old council of tribal elders finally sank into impotence before the rising power of the king (the situation seen in early historic Mesopotamia or among the Aztecs, for example [Adams 1966:139-142]), the time (possibly several generations earlier) at which the king had been only a war leader, holding his office temporarily at the pleasure of the council would no longer be remembered.

To provide ethnographic examples, it would be easy to imagine this sort of situation developing, under conditions of scarcity and "social circumscription," among the Yanomamö of Venezuela and Brazil, where villages defeated in warfare must seek the protection of stronger allies (see Chagnon 1968); or in Araucanian Chile, where neighboring dispersed settlements often united under an elected war leader (see Faron 1961).

There is another way in which intergroup cooperation among otherwise autonomous communities could lead to the gradual emergence of a single polity that embraced them all. Suttles (1960:303) hints at this in his discussion of the conversion of food into wealth among the Coast Salish: "If one community over a period of several years were to produce more food than its neighbors, it might come to have a greater part of the society's wealth." If that situation were to occur, there would seem to be three possible outcomes: (1) the system of exchanges might simply collapse; (2) a strategy such as potlatching might emerge to redistribute the wealth and hence allow the system to continue as it had in the past; or, (3) the group that had effectively monopolized the wealth might maintain its monopoly, or at least retain a more than proportionate share of the wealth, relying on some other mechanism to maintain inter-group exchange. If this wealth, once concentrated, could be manipulated in such a way as to promote the giving of tribute by other groups who wished to obtain part of it or to use it ceremonially (in the event that a supernatural quality were attached to certain items of wealth), then the area would be well on its way toward the chiefdom redistributive level, or even toward the minimal state level.

In more general terms, even without there being an actual wealth accumulation in the above sense, such an evolutionary advance could occur if one region became rather consistently more productive than the other regions with which it had cooperative alliances, simply because the ethics of reciprocity would induce a feeling of beholdenness on the part of the populations that consistently received more than they gave—and a corresponding feeling of *noblesse oblige* on the part of the group that most often ended up on the giving rather than the receiving end of the exchange. And any persistent attempt on the part of the group that rather consistently experienced scarcity to comply with the ethics of reciprocity by contributing *something*—be it labor, non-subsistence goods, or token amounts of one or a few selected foodstuffs —might well trigger the emergence of a chiefly redistributive system.

(7) Nothing in the above should be taken to mean that I deny that conflict and coercion have played a prominent role in sociocultural evolution. Carneiro's (this volume) and Webb's (1968) evidence suggests that warfare and conquest were definitely associated with the formation of large, strong states the world over. Perhaps warfare and conquest are indeed necessary conditions for the occurrence of that type of political organization. I would like to suggest, however, that focusing on the exceptional cases in social evolution—those cases of large state formation—may tend to obscure the operation of other evolutionary processes among the vast majority of peoples known to history and prehistory, who never achieved the state level.

It is important here to ask: At what point in the development of large states do we begin to find strong evidence of conquest warfare? As I have indicated, a chiefdom level of development could be reached rather gradually, without anyone's being killed or forcedly subjugated as a direct consequence. Perhaps conquest warfare is, in some cases at least, merely the final step in the formation of large states. Even at that, we should not forget that the occurrence of warfare does not preclude the possibility of the formation of alliances between victor and vanquished. Witness the intermarriage of the royal families of warring Europe—an example that is by no means exceptional in cross-cultural perspective.

(8) Because the major ethnographic material presented in this paper is drawn from non-agricultural areas, I wish to caution here that there may be something in the very nature of agriculture, particularly swidden agriculture, which could tip the scales in favor of conflict and conquest, as against cooperation (cf. Vayda 1961b). On the other hand, the literature is replete with examples of cooperative alliances among otherwise autonomous groups of swidden agriculturalists. Unless we take the view that these alliances occur largely for purposes of the exchange of sex partners, or simply because the "primitive" mind is titillated by inter-group contact, then we would appear to be forced to assume that they have some ecological importance. Incidentally, one of the most important features of agriculture is that it tends to cluster

resources; and if agriculturalists behave at all like non-agriculturalists, then the development or introduction of agriculture might well promote intergroup alliance and cooperation—perhaps at the same time promoting competition and conflict along some other dimensions.

Finally, I suggest that what is in order here is another thorough examination of "Cooperation and Competition among Primitive Peoples" (Mead 1937)—but this time from the standpoint of the mutual adjustments that human societies make in the process of extracting energy from their environments, rather than from the psychological viewpoint. If we are to be successful at this endeavor, we may need to abandon or seriously modify some of our most cherished anthropological ideas. I shall mention four of these in particular.

(1) We might profitably discard the notion that the Tribal and Chiefdom Levels of social organization are unlikely to emerge before the advent of agriculture.[9] The sophisticated techniques of the "new archaeology" are shedding increasing doubt on this assumption. We now have published evidence from a number of sites in the Near East indicating permanent settlements supported entirely by hunting and the collection of wild food (see Perrot 1960; van Loon 1966). And information from colleagues as well as from the popular press indicates that Northwestern University Professor Stuart Struever's excavations in Illinois have recently yielded strong evidence there of settled village life in the absence of agriculture. We may expect more of these instances to come to light, indicating that our evaluation of the importance of agriculture to sociocultural evolution has been faulty, at least in emphasis.

We have tended to think of agriculture in terms of its potential for creating large food surpluses, or at least food resources in unprecedented amounts; whereas it is entirely possible that the major importance of agriculture, at least in its early stages of development, is merely that it concentrates resources, establishing or enhancing tendencies for both inter-group cooperation and inter-group conflict (cf. Harner 1970). In areas where wild resources were already tightly clustered, sociocultural evolution easily could have proceeded to the chiefdom level in the absence of agriculture. We will probably discover more and more instances of this as our science, and particularly that branch called archaeology, becomes more sophisticated.

(2) We will probably have to modify our notion that universal evolution can be viewed profitably as having moved through four successive but analytically discrete levels: band, tribe, chiefdom, and state levels (see footnote 9). This analytical pigeon-holing may obscure the

mechanisms of sociocultural evolution. To begin with, all bands have some ties with other bands, and the usual situation is for these ties to lead to a congregation of bands for at least a short time each year. At the moment when they come together to cooperate in some activity (be it only eating together), are they so many separate "bands," or do they at that moment constitute a "tribe"? I think our tendency has been to strive for categorical neatness and largely to ignore the fact that our analytical categories do not reflect (and in fact, often deny) the empirical reality of at least some part of the annual round.

An equally thorny problem occurs in the distinction between chiefdom and state. If a strong chief temporarily succeeds in persuading his subjects to make *their* problems the *polity's* problems as well, to be resolved through adjudication rather than through direct retaliation, does he then head a "chiefdom," or does he then head a "state"? Again, we tend to strive for neatness, ignoring the possibility that the necessity for cooperation or the exigencies of competition in the exploitation of an environment may vest in the chief a virtual monopoly on the legitimate use of force—the hallmark of the state level—during part of the year.

The difference between the band and the tribe is a quantitative one; it is a difference in the relative strength of ties among groups that are residentially separate during part, or even most, of the year. The difference between the chiefdom and the state is also a quantitative one; it is a difference in the relative extent of the authority and power of the highest office holder(s). The difference between tribe and chiefdom, however, is a qualitative one; it is the difference between a non-institutionalized polity and an institutionalized polity, between a non-hierarchical and an hierarchical arrangement of component social units, between mechanical and organic solidarity. This distinction we must keep forever in mind, because of its broad implication for the organization of the labor force and the distribution of resources. But regarding the other analytical distinctions we commonly make, I suggest we begin speaking merely of weak or strong tribes and weak or strong states.[10] This change in the categories of analysis would highlight, or at least not obscure, the fact that the extent of cohesion within each of these two broad categories (tribes and states) may be and often is subject to seasonal and situational variations that occur because men organized in society have not just one, but a variety of strategies for exploiting the ever changing potentialities of their environment (see Gearing 1962, on "structural pose").

(3) We may have to shift our emphasis in field work. We need to investigate closely not only observable social relations and the observable flow of material goods or people per se, but also how people cognize their environment, and particularly, how they perceive their relations to other groups of people with whom they come into contact as they exploit their environment. This amounts to investigating the manner in which men organized in society arrive at their various strategies for exploiting their environment, whether in conjunction with or in competition with other such groups. We may need to ask some really naive questions: Why *don't* you marry your sister?[11] Why *don't* you simply massacre village X early some morning when they're all asleep? This line of inquiry may help us to delimit better the conditions under which one strategy or another is most likely to be followed, at present and through time.

(4) We may need to recast the whole problem, taking it out of the framework of "cooperation and competition" and putting it squarely in the more general framework of "adaptation." Perhaps cultural anthropology is presently at the same stage that biology was at during the last century, when nature was red in tooth and claw. Perhaps we, like the biologists, will come to speak more and more in adaptational terms, rather than in such shopworn and loaded terms as conflict and competition. It has been pointed out that an emphasis on cooperative models of social evolution ". . . sounds good and also appeals nicely to our American prejudice toward cooperation and constitutionalism" (Webb 1968:2). Perhaps we have an equally strong tendency in the opposite direction, one that appeals to another Anglo-American prejudice—competition.

NOTES

[1]This essay is a modified version of a paper presented at the American Anthropological Association Annual Meeting in New York, November 1971. I have profited greatly from the suggestions of two of my former students, Alred M. Lee and Walter Precourt. Others who have provided encouragement or criticism are Ivan Brady, Gustav Carlson, Beth Dillingham, Robert Foist, Arthur Hinman, Frederick McEvoy, Elman Service, Thomas Settlemyre, Albert Spaulding, and Malcolm Webb.

At the outset, it should be noted that a truly adequate cross-cultural definition of "surplus" and "scarcity" is difficult to formulate, because it would have to include both objectively measurable and subjective features. True, we can define a minimal biophysical subsistence level at which there is a thermodynamic equilibrium of energy input and output, and below which a population would perish (Harris 1959:190). No society could operate long at this bare level, however, because the reproductive and socializational activities necessary to transgenerational survival of the society and its culture would be impaired. Thus, as Harris (1959:190) has pointed out, "all viable societies produce food in greater abundance than is necessary for mere biological thermodynamic equilibrium. In this sense, every society produces a 'surplus above subsistence'." What we encounter empirically are variations in the amount of energy produced above this bare subsistence level so defined. Scarcity and surplus are relative in the qualitative sense, also; like beauty, they are at least partly in the eye of the beholder. A thorough discussion of the concepts of surplus and scarcity can be found in Pearson (1957), Harris (1959), Dalton (1960), and Orans (1966).

For purposes of this paper, the terms will be used in the following absolute and relative senses. *Scarcity* means either: (a) *biophysical scarcity*, in which food supply is currently at or lower than the minimal biophysical subsistence level (the society is not viable); or, (b) *relative scarcity*, in which food supply is perceived as currently lower than previously (it may or may not be low enough to threaten sociocultural continuity). *Surplus* means either: (a) *biophysical surplus*, in which food supply is currently greater than the biophysical subsistence requirement (all viable societies have a surplus in this sense); or, (b) *relative surplus*, in which food supply is perceived as currently greater than before.

²For a discussion of other forces or factors that have been considered prime-movers of evolution, see the selections by Service and Carneiro in this volume. The best single work on universal evolution is Leslie A. White's *The Evolution of Culture* (1959b).

³I am not repeating here Martin Orans' (1966) incisive criticism of this debate, because I feel that the more recent articles by Carneiro (this volume) and Harner (1970) have largely superceded the points raised by Orans.

⁴Woodburn (1968:52) makes a similar point regarding the hunting-gathering Hadza of Tanzania. As Binford (1968:328) has pointed out, recent data on several primitive societies lay to rest the familiar notion ". . . that cultural elaboration is caused by leisure time which is available for the first time to agriculturalists." All recent evidence seems to support Service (1966:13) in his statement that ". . . the more primitive the culture the more leisured will be the people. . . ."

⁵In some other places and times a per capita decrease in food supply appears to have been a precipitating cause of the development of agriculture (see White 1959b:283-287; and this volume). At present, the Bushmen do not face such a situation. Lee (1968:33) asked a Bushman why they hadn't taken up agriculture, and got the reply: "Why should we plant, when there are so many mongongo nuts in the world?" Interestingly, there is some evidence to suggest that agriculture may be less adaptive than hunting and gathering in this area over the long run. During the drought that was occurring while Lee was on the scene, the agricultural-pastoral Herero and Tswana women ". . . were able to feed their families only by joining the Bushman women to forage for wild foods" (Lee 1968:40). We should note that the Tswana and Herero are relatively latecomers to this region who brought with them an agricultural-pastoral way of life that had evolved under quite different circumstances.

⁶This seems quite reasonable in light of the truly dramatic increase in infanticide in Europe during the period 1750-1850, when population there nearly doubled. As late as 1878, some 6% of all violent deaths in England were infanticides (see Langer 1972).

⁷Ireland provides an instance in which a quick decimation resulted in a drastically altered family structure designed to reduce fertility. Before the great potato famine, which began in 1845, the Irish married early and had large families (Langer 1972:99). After the famine, which over a ten-year period reduced the population by 20% through death and emigration, marriage for males was greatly delayed and many females never married. As

late as 1901, some 22% of all women in the age-group 45-54 were still single (Wrigley 1969:10, 165). For a general discussion of control and spacing mechanisms in human populations, see Birdsell (1971).

[8]It is interesting that this feature of the surplus theory is integrated into Carneiro's scarcity model (cf. Orans 1966).

[9]In speaking of levels of social organization, I am following Service (1963:xx-xxix). A Band is a small, unstratified family group. A Tribe, which is also unstratified, might be viewed as a congeries of bands. Neither the band nor the tribe has political offices as such; leadership is ephemeral and largely ad hoc. A chiefdom is a stratified, hierarchically organized society in which authority is continuously exercised from at least one political office (the chieftaincy). The major difference between a chiefdom and a state is that only in the latter does some person, body, or office have a monopoly on the legitimate use of force within the polity.

[10]After I presented a version of this paper at the 1971 American Anthropological Association Meeting, it was brought to my attention that Service, who was instrumental in defining these four analytical levels, has recently proposed much the same thing that I am proposing here (Service 1968b:167; and 1971: Ch. 10; see also Fried 1967:164-184).

[11]I have heard it said that one senior anthropologist once did, in fact, ask this question, and that the response was: "Why waste a marriage?"

BIBLIOGRAPHY

Adams, Robert M.
1955.   "Developmental Stages in Ancient Mesopotamia." In *Irrigation Civilizations: A Comparative Study*, edited by J. Steward, pp. 6-18. Washington, D.C.: Pan American Union.
1960.   "Early Civilizations, Subsistence, and Environment." In *City Invincible*, edited by C. Kraeling and R. Adams, pp. 269-295. Chicago: University of Chicago Press.
1962.   "Agriculture and Urban Life in Early Southwestern Iran." *Science* 136:109-22.
1966.   *The Evolution of Urban Society*. Chicago: Aldine.
Allport, G. W.
1947.   "Guidelines for Research in International Cooperation." *Journal of Social Issues* 3:21-37.
Bagehot, Walter
1873.   *Physics and Politics*. New York: D. Appleton and Co.
Barnes, Harry Elmer
1960.   "Foreword." In *Essays in the Science of Culture in Honor of Leslie A. White*, edited by G. Dole and R. Carneiro, xi-xlvi. New York: Thomas Y. Crowell.
Barnett, Homer G.
1940.   "Culture Processes." *American Anthropologist* 42:21-48.
1953.   *Innovation: The Basis of Cultural Change*. New York: McGraw-Hill.
1965.   "Laws of Socio-Cultural Change." *International Journal of Comparative Sociology* 6:207-30.
Bassett, Raymond E.
1946.   "Letter to Editor." *Science* 103:25-26.
Benjamin, Park
1901.   *The Age of Electricity*. New York: C. Scribner's Sons.
Berreman, Gerald D.
1966.   "Anemic and Emetic Analyses in Social Anthropology," *American Anthropologist* 68:346-54.

Binford, L. R.
   1968.   "Post-Pleistocene Adaptations." In *New Perspectives in Archeology*, edited by S. and L. Binford, pp. 313-41. Chicago: Aldine.
Birdsell, Joseph B.
   1971.   "Australia: Ecology, Spacing Mechanisms and Adaptive Behaviour in Aboriginal Land Tenure." In *Land Tenure in the Pacific*, edited by R. Crocombe, pp. 334-61. Melbourne: Oxford University Press.
Boas, Franz
   1911.   "Introduction." In *Handbook of American Indian Languages*, edited by F. Boas, pp. 5-83. Washington, D.C.: Smithsonian Institution, Bureau of American Ethnology, Bull. 40, Pt. 1.
   1940.   "The Methods of Ethnology." In *Race, Language and Culture*, F. Boas, pp. 281-89. New York: MacMillan.
Braidwood, Robert J.
   1948.   *Prehistoric Men*. Chicago: Chicago Natural History Museum.
Braidwood, Robert J., and Linda Braidwood
   1949.   "On the Treatment of the Prehistoric Near Eastern Materials in Steward's 'Cultural Causality and Law'." *American Anthropologist* 51:665-69.
Braidwood, Robert J., and Charles A. Reed
   1957.   "The Achievement and Early Consequences of Food-Production: A Consideration of the Archaeological and Natural-Historical Evidence." *Cold Spring Harbor Symposia on Quantitative Biology*, 22:, 19-31. New York: Long Island Biological Association.
Brinton, Crane
   1952.   *The Anatomy of Revolution*. Rev. ed. New York: Prentice-Hall.
Burling, Robbins
   1964.   "Cognition and Componential Analysis: God's Truth or Hocus-Pocus?" *American Anthropologist* 66:20-28.
Carneiro, Robert L.
   1958.   "Agriculture and the Beginning of Civilization." *Ethnographisch-archäolische Forschungen* 4:22-27.
   1960.   "Slash-and-Burn Agriculture: A Closer Look at Its Implications for Settlement Patterns." In *Men and Cultures*, edited by A. Wallace, pp. 229-34. Philadelphia: University of Pennsylvania Press.
   1961.   "Slash-and-Burn Cultivation Among the Kuikuru and Its Implication for Cultural Development in the Amazon Basin." In *Evolution of Horticultural Systems in Native South America: A Symposium*, edited by J. Wilbert, pp. 47-67. Caracas: Sociedad de Ciencias Naturales La Salle.
   1962.   "Scale Analysis as an Instrument for the Study of Cultural Evolution." *Southwestern Journal of Anthropology* 18:149-69.

1967.   *The Evolution of Society; Selections from Herbert Spencer's Principles of Sociology.* Chicago: University of Chicago Press.
1970.   "A Theory of the Origin of the State." *Science* 169:733-38.
Chagnon, Napoleon A.
1968.   *Yanomamö, The Fierce People.* New York: Holt, Rinehart & Winston.
1970.   "The Culture-Ecology of Shifting (Pioneering) Cultivation among the Yanomamö Indians." *Proceedings of the 8th International Congress of Anthropological and Ethnological Sciences,* 3:249-55. Tokyo and Kyoto.
Childe, V. Gordon
1936.   *Man Makes Himself.* London: Watts.
1946.   *What Happened in History.* New York: Pelican.
1950.   "The Urban Revolution." *The Town Planning Review* 21:3-17.
Coe, M. D.
1966.   *The Maya.* New York: Praeger.
Dalton, George
1960.   "A Note of Clarification on Economic Surplus." *American Anthropologist* 62:483-90.
de la Vega, Garcilaso
1966.   *Royal Commentaries on the Incas and General History of Peru, Part I,* translated by H. Livermore. Austin: University of Texas Press.
Denevan, W.
1966.   "The Aboriginal Cultural Geography of the Llanos de Mojos of Bolivia." *Ibero-Americana* 48.
Drucker, Phillip, and Robert F. Heizer
1967.   *To Make My Name Good: A Reexamination of the Southern Kwakiutl Potlatch.* Berkeley and Los Angeles: University of California Press.
Durkheim, Emile
1897.   *Le Suicide.* Paris: Félix Alcan.
1915.   *The Elementary Forms of Religious Life,* translated by J. Swain. London: Allen & Unwin.
1933.   *The Division of Labor in Society.* London: The Free Press of Glencoe, Collier-MacMillan Ltd.
1938.   *The Rules of Sociological Method,* translated by S. Solvay and J. Meuller. Chicago: University of Chicago Press.
Engels, Friedrich
1883.   "Speech at the Graveside of Karl Marx." In *Karl Marx: Selected Works,* edited by V. Adoratsky. Moscow: Co-Operative Publishing Society of Foreign Workers in the USSR.
1942.   *The Origin of the Family, Private Property, and the State.* New York: International Publishers.

1961.   "Socialism, Utopian and Scientific." In *Essential Works of Marxism*, edited by A. Mendel, pp. 45-82. New York: Bantam.

Faron, Louis C.
1961.   *Mapuche Social Structure*. Urbana: University of Illinois Press.

Ferdon, Edwin M., Jr.
1959.   "Agricultural Potential and the Development of Culture." *Southwestern Journal of Anthropology* 15:1-19.

Field, Stanley
1943.   "Fifty Years of Progress." *Field Museum News*, 14.

Flannery, Kent V.
1965.   "The Ecology of Early Food Production in Mesopotamia." *Science* 147:1247-56.

Fock, Niels
1964.   "Man as a Mediating Agent between Nature and Culture." *Folk* 6:47-53.

Frank, L. K.
1944.   "What Is Social Order?" *American Journal of Sociology* 49:470-77.

Fried, Morton
1960.   "On the Evolution of Social Stratification and the State." In *Culture in History*, edited by S. Diamond, pp. 713-31. New York: Columbia University Press.

1967.   *The Evolution of Political Society*. New York: Random House.

Gearing, Fred
1962.   *Priests and Warriors: Social Structures for Cherokee Politics in the Eighteenth Century*. Washington, D.C.: American Anthropological Association Memoir No. 93.

Geertz, Clifford
1957.   "Ritual and Social Change: A Javanese Example." *American Anthropologist* 59:32-54.

1962.   "The Growth of Culture and the Evolution of Mind." In *Theories of the Mind*, edited by J. Scher, pp. 713-40.

1963.   *Agricultural Involution: The Process of Ecological Change in Indonesia*. Berkeley: University of California Press.

1966.   "Religion as a Cultural System." In *Anthropological Approaches to the Study of Religion*, edited by M. Banton, pp. 1-46. Association for Social Anthropology Monograph 3. New York: Praeger.

Gernet, Jacques
1968.   *Ancient China: From the Beginnings to the Empire*, translated by R. Rudoff. London: Faber and Faber.

Goodenough, Ward
1964.   "Cultural Anthropology and Linguistics." In *Language in Culture and Society*, edited by D. Hymes, pp. 36-39. New York: Harper & Row.

1971.   "Culture, Language and Society." *McCaleb Module in Anthropology*. Reading, Mass.: Addison-Wesley.

Griffin, James B.
1967.   "Eastern North American Archaeology: A Summary." *Science* 156:
         175-91.
Gumplowicz, Ludwig
1883.   *Der Rassenkampf*. Innsbruck: Wagner.
Hammel, Eugene A., and William S. Simmons, eds.
1970.   *Man Makes Sense*. Boston: Little, Brown and Co.
Harlan, Jack R.
1971.   "Agricultural Origins: Centers and Noncenters." *Science* 174:468-
         74.
Harner, Michael J.
1970.   "Population Pressure and the Social Evolution of Agricultural-
         ists." *Southwestern Journal of Anthropology* 26:67-86.
Harris, Marvin
1959.   "The Economy Has No Surplus?" *American Anthropologist*
         61:185-99.
1964.   *The Nature of Cultural Things*. New York: Random House.
1968.   *The Rise of Anthropological Theory*. New York: Crowell.
1969.   "Monistic Determinism: Anti-Service." *Southwestern Journal of
         Anthropology* 25:198-206.
Huxley, Sir Julian S.
1955.   "Evolution, Biological and Cultural." In *Yearbook of Anthropol-
         ogy*, pp. 3-25. New York: Wenner-Gren Foundation for Anthropo-
         logical Research.
Hymes, Dell, ed.
1964.   *Language in Culture and Society*. New York, Evanston and Lon-
         don: Harper and Row.
James, William
1880.   "Great Men, Great Thoughts and the Environment." *Atlantic
         Monthly* 46:441-59.
1890.   "The Importance of Individuals." *The Open Court* 4:2437-40.
Jeans, James, *et al.*
1931.   *Essays in Living Philosophies*. New York.
Jenks, E.
1900.   *A History of Politics*. New York: Macmillan.
Kardiner, Abram, and Edward Preble
1963.   *They Studied Man*. New York: Mentor.
Kenyon, Kathleen M.
1959.   "Some Observations on the Beginnings of Settlement in the Near
         East." *Journal of the Royal Anthropological Institute of Great
         Britain and Ireland* 89:35-43.
Kroeber, Alfred L.
1917.   "The Superorganic." *American Anthropologist* 19:163-213.
1919.   "On the Principle of Order in Civilization as Exemplified by
         Changes in Fashion." *American Anthropologist* 21:235-63.

1939.   *Cultural and Natural Areas of Native North America.* Berkeley: University of California Press

Kroeber, Alfred L., and Clyde Kluckhohn
1952.   "Culture: A Critical Review of Concepts and Definitions." *Papers of the Peabody Museum,* Harvard University, vol. 47.

Kroeber, Alfred L., and Jane Richardson
1940.   "Three Centuries of Women's Dress Fashions: A Quantitative Analysis." *Anthropological Records* (Berkeley) 5:111-54.

Kushner, Gilbert, *et al.*
1962.   *What Accounts for Sociocultural Change? A Propositional Inventory.* Chapel Hill: University of North Carolina Press.

Langer, William L.
1972.   "Checks on Population Growth: 1750-1850." *Scientific American* 226:93-99.

Lanning, E. P.
1967.   *Peru before the Incas.* Englewood Cliffs, N.J.: Prentice-Hall.

Lee, Richard B.
1968.   "What Hunters Do for a Living, or How to Make Out on Scarce Resources." In *Man the Hunter,* edited by R. Lee and I. DeVore, pp. 30-48. Chicago: Aldine.
1969.   "!Kung Bushman Subsistence: An Input-Output Analysis." *Environment and Cultural Behavior,* edited by A. Vayda, pp. 47-79. Garden City, N.Y.: Natural History Press.

Lee, Richard B., and Irven DeVore
1968.   "Problems in the Study of Hunters and Gatherers." In *Man the Hunter,* edited by R. Lee and I. DeVore, pp. 3-12 Chicago: Aldine.

Lévi-Strauss, Claude
1963.   *Structural Anthropology,* translated by C. Jacobson and B. Schoepf. New York and London: Basic Books.
1964.   *Tristes Tropiques,* translated by J. Russel. New York: Atheneum.

Linton, Ralph
1936.   *The Study of Man.* New York: D. Appleton-Century Co.

Lowie, Robert H.
1940.   *An Introduction to Cultural Anthropology.* Rev. ed. New York: Rinehart & Co., Inc.

Malinowski, Bronislaw
1922.   *Argonauts of the Western Pacific.* New York: Dutton.
1926.   *Crime and Custom in Savage Society.* London: Kegan Paul.

Mangelsdorf, Paul C.
1958.   "Reconstructing the Ancestor of Corn." *Science* 128:1313-20.

Mangelsdorf, Paul C., *et al.*
1964.   "Domestication of Corn." *Science* 143:538-45.

Mead, Margaret ed.
1937.   *Cooperation and Competition among Primitive Peoples.* New

York: McGraw-Hill.

Meggers, Betty J.
1954.   "Environmental Limitations on the Development of Culture."
         American Anthropologist 56:801-24.

Merton, Robert
1961.   "Singleton and Multiples in Scientific Discovery: A Chapter in
         the Sociology of Science." *Proceedings of the American Philosoph-
         ical Society* 105:470-86.

Morgan, Lewis Henry
1877.   *Ancient Society.* New York: World Publishing Co.
1963.   *Ancient Society,* edited by E. Leacock. Cleveland and New York:
         Meridian Books.

Morley, S. G., and G. W. Brainerd
1956.   *The Ancient Maya.* 3rd ed. Stanford: Stanford University Press.

Naroll, Raoul
1956.   "A Preliminary Index of Social Development." *American Anthro-
         pologist* 58:687-715.

Ogburn, William F.
1922.   *Social Change.* New York: The Viking Press.

Ogburn, William F., and Dorothy Thomas
1922.   "Are Inventions Inevitable? A Note on Social Evolution." *Politi-
         cal Science Quarterly* 37:83-98.

Oppenheimer, Franz
1926.   *The State,* translated by J. Gitterman. New York: Vanguard.

Orans, Martin
1966.   "Surplus." *Human Organization* 25:24-32.

Otterbein, Keith
1970.   *The Evolution of War.* New Haven: Human Relations Area Files
         Press.

Pearson, Harry
1957.   "The Economy Has No Surplus." In *Trade and Market in the
         Early Empires,* edited by K. Polanyi, C. Arensberg, and H. Pear-
         son, pp. 320-41. Glencoe, Ill.: Free Press.

Perrot, Jean
1960.   "Excavations at Eyhan (Ain Mallaha)." *The Israel Exploration
         Journal* 10:14-22

Piddocke, Stuart
1965.   "The Potlatch System of the Southern Kwakiutl: A New Perspec-
         tive." *Southwestern Journal of Anthropology* 21:244-64.

Pospisil, Leonard
1958.   "Social Change and Primitive Law: Consequences of a Papuan
         Papuan Legal Case." *American Anthropologist* 60:832-37.

Puleston, D. E., and D. W. Callender
1967.   "Defense Earthworks at Tikal." *Expedition* 9:40-48.

Ratzenhofer, Gustav
    1893.   *Wesen und Zweck der Politik.* Leipsig: Brockhaus.
Reed, Charles A.
    1959.   "Animal Domestication in the Prehistoric Near East." *Science* 130:
             1629-39.
Sahlins, Marshall, and Elman Service, eds.
    1960.   *Evolution and Culture.* Ann Arbor: University of Michigan Press.
Schmidt, W.
    1939.   *The Culture Historical Method of Ethnology,* translated by S. Sie-
             ber. New York: Fortuny's.
Schneider, David M.
    1968.   *American Kinship: A Cultural Account.* Englewood Cliffs, N.J.:
             Prentice-Hall.
Service, Elman R.
    1963.   *Profiles in Ethnology.* New York: Harper & Row.
    1966.   *The Hunters.* Englewood Cliffs, N.J.: Prentice-Hall.
    1968a.   "The Prime-Mover of Cultural Evolution." *Southwestern Journal
             of Anthropology* 24:396-409.
    1968b   "War and Our Contemporary Ancestors." In *War: The Anthro-
             pology of Armed Conflict and Agression,* edited by M. Fried, M.
             Harris, and R. Murphy, pp. 160-67. Garden City, N.Y.: Double-
             day and Co., Natural History Press.
    1969.   "Models for the Methodology of Mouthtalk." *Southwestern Jour-
             nal of Anthropology* 25:68-80.
    1971.   *Cultural Evolutionism: Theory in Practice.* New York: Holt, Rine-
             hart and Winston.
Sieber, Sylvester A., S.J., and Franz H. Mueller, M.C.S.
    1941.   *The Social Life of Primitive Man.* St. Louis, Mo., and London:
             B. Herder Book Co.
Solheim, Wilhelm G., II
    1972.   "An Earlier Agricultural Revolution." *Scientific American* 226:
             34-41.
Steward, Julian H.
    1930.   "Irrigation without Agriculture." *Papers, Michigan Academy of
             Science, Arts and Letters* 12:149-56.
    1949.   "Cultural Causality and Law: A Trial Formulation of the Develop-
             ment of Early Civilizations." *American Anthropologist* 51:1-27.
    1955.   *Theory of Culture Change.* Urbana: University of Illinois Press.
    1960.   *Review of: "The Evolution of Culture," by Leslie A. White. Amer-
             ican Anthropologist* 62:144-48.
Suttles, Wayne
    1960.   "Affinal Ties, Subsistence, and Prestige among the Coast Salish."
             American Anthropologist 62:296-305.

1968. "Coping with Abundance: Subsistence on the Northwest Coast." In *Man the Hunter*, edited by R. Lee and I. Devore, pp. 56-68. Chicago: Aldine.

Taine, Hippolyte Adolphe
1863. *Historie de la Littérature Anglaise, Vol. I.* Paris: Librairie Hachette.

Tatje, Terrance A., and Raoul Naroll
1970. "Two Measures of Societal Complexity: An Empirical Cross-Cultural Comparison." In *A Handbook of Method in Cultural Anthropology*, edited by R. Naroll and R. Cohen, Ch. 40. Garden City, N.Y.: Doubleday and Co., Natural History Press.

Thomas, Elizabeth Marshall
1965. *The Harmless People.* New York: Vintage Books.

Thurston, R. H.
1902. *A History of the Growth of the Steam Engine.* 4th ed., rev. New York: D. Appleton & Co.

Tylor, E. B.
1871. *Primitive Culture.* 5th ed. (1929 printing). London: John Murray.

van Loon, Maurits N.
1966. "Mureybat: An Early Village in Inland Syria." *Archaeology* 19: 215-16.

Vansina, Jan
1966. *Kingdoms of the Savanna.* Madison: University of Wisconsin Press.

Vayda, Andrew P.
1961a. "A Re-Examination of Northwest Coast Economic Systems." *Transactions of the New York Academy of Science (Series 2)* 23:618-24.

1961b. "Expansion and Warfare among Swidden Agriculturalists." *American Anthropologist* 63:346-58.

1967. "Pomo Trade Feasts." In *Tribal and Peasant Economies*, edited by G. Dalton, pp. 494-500. Garden City, N.Y.: Doubleday and Co., Natural History Press.

Ward, Lester F.
1883. *Dynamic Sociology, Vol. 2.* New York: Appleton.

Webb, Malcolm C.
1968. "Carneiro's Hypothesis of Limited Land Resources and the Origins of the State: A Latin Americanist's Approach to an Old Problem." *South Eastern Latin Americanist* 12:1-8

Westgate, Lewis G.
1943. "Man's Long Story." *Scientific Monthly* 57:155-65.

White, Leslie A.
1947. "Culturological *vs.* Psychological Interpretations of Human Behavior." *American Sociological Review* 12:686-98.

1949. *The Science of Culture.* New York: Farrar, Straus and Cudahy.

154   *A Reader in the ...*

1959a. "The Concept of (

1959b. *The Evolution c*

1969. "Preface to th
L. A. White,
Giroux.

White, Leslie A., an

1973. *The Co*

Whitehead, Alfre

1933. *Science a.*
University Press.

Wissler, Clark

1923. *Man and Culture*. New York.

Wittfogel, Karl

1957. *Oriental Despotism*. New Haven: Yale U..

Woodburn, James

1968. "An Introduction to Hadza Ecology." In *Man the Hu..*
by R. Lee and I. DeVore, pp. 49-55. Chicago: Aldine.

Wrigley, E. A.

1969. *Population and History*. New York and Toronto: McGraw-Hill.